START SPINNING

Everything You Need to Know to Make Great Yarn

MAGGIE CASEY

Cover and interior design, Laura Shaw Design Inc.
Text © 2008 by Maggie Casey. Photography and illustrations © Interweave Press LLC, 2008
All rights reserved.

interweavebooks.com

Interweave Press LLC, 201 East Fourth Street, Loveland, CO 80537-5655 USA
Printed in China through Asia Pacific Offset.

Library of Congress Cataloging-in-Publication Data
Casey, Maggie, 1943-
Start spinning : everything you need to know to make great yarn /
Maggie Casey, author.
p. cm.
Includes bibliographical references and index.
ISBN-13: 978-1-59668-065-4 (pbk.)
1. Hand spinning. 2. Spun yarns. I. Title.
TT847.C35 2008
746.1'2--dc22   2007036774

10 9 8 7 6 5 4 3 2

TABLE OF CONTENTS

Why spin?

Why should the ancient craft of spinning be so appealing today? We don't need to spin to clothe ourselves when a quick trip to the nearest shopping center offers a world of choices. We no longer travel on ships with handspun sails controlled by handspun rope. Why, then, are we so drawn to spinning?

Spinning is the thread that connects us to our past. In many creation stories, spinning plays a crucial role: Spider Woman brought spinning to the Navajo. Myths and legends and fairy tales are full of spinning references. In Greek mythology, Arachne challenged the goddess Athena to a spinning contest, lost, and was turned into a spider. Then there are the three Fates, who spin the thread of life, measure it out, and decide when to cut it off. As children, we fell asleep hearing about *Sleeping Beauty*, who pricked her finger on a spinning wheel, and Rumpelstilskin, who spun straw into gold.

Today we don't need to spin our own yarn, but the wonderful thing is that we *can*. And when we do, a new world opens to us. We can choose the fiber. Do you want wool, silk, or mohair? What kind of wool—Merino soft or Lincoln strong? What about linen or cotton or the new fibers like Soysilk or bamboo? We can spin a yarn that is fat or thin, soft or firm. We can spin a single strand or many plies. We can dye the fiber before it is spun or dye the finished yarn. We can spin the yarn of our dreams!

Spinning is the simple process of pulling out fibers and adding twist. That is all it is: a very simple process with a world of variation.

All it takes is fluff, a spindle or wheel, and patience.

CHAPTER ONE

Start with Wool

The world is full of exciting, exotic fibers from lustrous, smooth silk to soft, buttery cashmere. Plants give us sturdy linen and fine cotton, and don't forget soy, bamboo, and corn fibers. All of these fibers make beautiful, useful yarns, but wool is the easiest fiber to spin and the best one to learn with.

Crimpy locks of wool

WHY WOOL?

Even spinners who can make yarn with ease from slippery silk or short-fibered cotton often prefer to spin wool because of its unique properties. When wool is spun into yarn, air spaces become trapped by the twist. These air spaces act like a double-paned window and make wool a good insulator. Wool is absorbent; it can absorb thirty percent of its weight in water before it feels wet, which is why wool mittens keep your hands warm and dry even after a snowball fight. Like other protein fibers, wool is fire-resistant. Wool will burn if a flame is held to it but will self-extinguish once the flame is removed.

You can make a wool yarn as soft as a feather or as strong as a rope—it just depends on the breed of sheep you choose. There are many different breeds of sheep and great variety in their wool, but all wools share some common traits.

If you look at a **lock** or **staple** of wool (a small bundle or clump of wool fibers within a fleece), the first thing you notice is the **crimp** (the waviness of the wool fiber). Crimp varies with the breed of sheep. Fine wools such as Merino have a fine fiber with lots of crimp, as many as 30 crimps per inch (2.5 cm). Coarser wools like Wensleydale have thicker fibers and much less crimp. Crimp gives wool its elasticity; you can stretch wool out and when you let it go, it pops back into shape. It is the reason a wool skirt or suit looks crisp and holds its shape. This stretchiness allows wool to resist abrasion and remain strong. Wool yarn's elasticity is also what makes it the first choice for beginning knitters; the bounce balances out uneven tension in the stitches. You will also notice the length of the group of fibers, commonly called the **staple length**. Staple length describes a fiber's average length. The staple length of cotton is very short—about 1 inch (2.5 cm)—while a long wool might have a staple length of 6–8 inches (15–20.5 cm). The term originally applied to a lock of wool, but now it is also used to describe other fibers. Knowing the staple length of a fiber makes it easier to draft and spin. To find staple length, measure the length of a few fibers that you pull out and examine. When you draft a long fiber, your hands will need to be farther apart than when drafting a short fiber. Medium-length fibers (3–5 inches or 7.5–12.5 cm) are generally easiest to spin, especially in the beginning.

If you looked at a wool fiber under a microscope, you would see small overlapping scales like the bracts on a pinecone. These scales, known as the **cuticle**, grab on to one another in the spinning process and make a strong yarn. They are also the reason why wool felts.

Wool is widely available and renewable—there are wool festivals all over the world; the ads in *Spin-Off* magazine offer lots of choices; your local yarn shop may carry spinning fiber; and there is always the Internet.

Overlapping scales on wool fiber

START FROM THE SHEEP

Spinning fleece you have prepared is the best, like eating your own homegrown, fresh-picked strawberries. A yarn spun from a hand-prepared fleece has more character than yarn spun from commercially prepared fiber. It is the difference between those homegrown strawberries and the frozen ones from the grocery store: both are delicious, but homegrown berries rule!

Don't worry; just because you prepare the fleece doesn't mean

Learning to spin on fleece you have prepared is the best, like eating your own homegrown, fresh-picked strawberries.

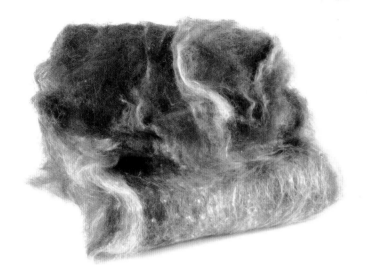

Batt

Sliver

Roving

Combed Top

you have to raise the sheep. You can find fleece at wool festivals and many county fairs, check out the ads in *Spin-Off,* or ask at your local yarn shop. If your shop doesn't sell fleece, they may know of someone in the area who raises sheep for handspinners. If you have a weavers' guild in your area, they too may know of someone who has a spinners' flock. For detailed directions on the delightful process of preparing your own fiber, see page 94.

COMMERCIALLY PREPARED FIBERS

When you buy fibers that have been commercially prepared, all the hard work has been done for you. The fiber has been washed, then *carded* or *combed.* Carded fibers are usually shorter (less than 4 inches [10 cm]) and include all the fibers, long and short. Most of the fibers go in the same direction, but the preparation is not completely smooth and even. Traditionally, combed fibers are usually longer, all the short fibers have been removed, and the combing process lines up the fibers in an even, dense formation.

Carded preparations are usually easier to spin because the fibers are more open and they pull out or draft easily. Beginning spinners should choose carded fiber.

TYPES OF PREPARED FIBER

§   *Rolags* are small rolls of fiber prepared on handcards. (See page 103 for directions on using handcards and making rolags.)

§   A *batt* is a rectangle of carded fibers just as it comes off a drum carder.

§   *Sliver* (pronounced "SLY-ver") is carded fiber that has been pulled out into a long strand.

§   *Roving* is carded and then drawn out into a long strand of overlapping fibers, sometimes with a little twist added. If you look at roving and sliver, the fibers will look more disorganized than those of combed top.

§   *Combed top* is also a long strand of fibers, but all the short fibers have been removed and the fibers are totally parallel. Top is very smooth, and the fibers are very close together.

When you buy fibers that have been commercially prepared, all the hard work has been done for you.

CHAPTER TWO

Things to Know Before You Spin

With fiber in hand, you're probably eager to start spinning right away. Before you start twisting your fiber into yarn, learn a few techniques and ideas that will help you understand the process better.

Pre-drafting

1. Gently pull some of the fibers so that they slip past each other but don't separate completely.

2. If you pull the ends apart too much, the roving will come apart.

3. If the roving breaks, overlap the broken ends.

4. Draft the broken ends together.

5. Wind the pre-drafted fibers into a loose "bird's nest."

DRAFTING

To make yarn, you first pull out, or **draft**, the fibers, then add twist. A spindle or a wheel will add the twist—that is the easy part—but it's up to you to draft out the fibers.

A little practice in drafting the fibers before you sit down at your wheel or pick up your spindle will help you get a feel for the process. Hold a rolag or small strip of carded fiber in one hand (the fiber hand) and use the other hand (the drafting hand) to start pulling some of the fibers out from one end. Don't pull them completely apart, but feel the fibers slip past one another. That's drafting. If you added twist now, you would make yarn.

Instead of adding twist, pull out or draft some more fibers; each time you draft the fibers you want to stop just before you pull them completely apart. (If you do pull them apart, don't fret; overlap the fibers and start drafting again.) If the fibers don't slip past one another, try holding your hands a little farther apart. Continue to work your drafting hand down the rolag or strip of fiber and gently pull those fibers out until they form a long strand of overlapping fibers. This technique is called **pre-drafting** and is sometime used to prepare fibers for spinning. After drafting out these fibers, you can loosely wind them into a "bird's nest" until you are ready to spin them.

Pull off about 6 inches (15 cm) of your pre-drafted fiber. This loose strand of fibers isn't strong; in fact a quick tug will pull it apart. To turn this strand into yarn, add a little twist with your drafting hand—all of a sudden the fibers can't slip past one another anymore. But if you relax and let a little more fiber out of your fiber hand, you can start drafting again. Spinning is the act of balancing these two actions—drafting the fibers and then adding enough twist so the fibers can no longer slip past one another. If you add too little twist, your yarn will fall apart; if you add too much, you won't be able to draft.

THE DRAFTING TRIANGLE

Yarn is created in the **drafting triangle**. This is the area where the twist meets the fiber and turns it into yarn. As the spinner drafts out the fibers, the twist engages the front ends of the fibers while the spinner keeps the tail ends under control. The number of fibers in the drafting triangle determines the size of the yarn: Many fibers create a bulky yarn, while few fibers make a fine yarn. The size of the triangle will change depending on the length of the fiber; silk has a very long triangle, and cotton has a very short one.

S- AND Z-TWIST

Yarns are described as having S- or Z-twist. It sounds quite odd, but it is just spinner's shorthand. Z-twist yarn is spun clockwise (to the right); S-twist is spun counterclockwise (to the left). In yarn spun to the right, the twist will slant in the same direction as the center stroke of the letter Z. The twist in yarn spun to the left has the same slant as the center of the letter S. The twist in a yarn slants in the same direction no matter which end of the yarn you look at.

Most yarns are spun with a Z-twist and then plied in the opposite direction, giving the finished yarn an S-twist. From a practical perspective, this means that when you spin, you will want the spindle or wheel to turn clockwise. When you ply, you will want the wheel or spindle to go in the opposite direction.

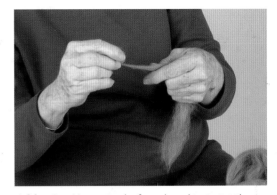

Add twist: Use your drafting hand to twist the fibers. With enough twist in the fibers, they cannot slip past each other anymore.

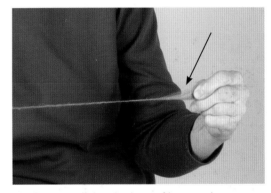

Drafting triangle: The loose fibers in the spinner's hand are twisted into yarn.

CHAPTER THREE

Spinning Yarn on a Spindle

Want to get in touch with the past? Learn to spin on a spindle. For most of history, all of the world's cloth was spindle spun. The wrappings of Egyptian mummies, the sails of the Viking explorers, and the fine robes described in the Bible were all spun on a spindle. A spinning wheel may be faster, but a spindle is portable and inexpensive.

Spindles can be
rustic and plain
or elegant and exotic.

SPINDLE ANATOMY

Most spindles are composed of a spindle shaft and a whorl. The spindle shafts are usually hardwood, but other materials can be used as long as the shaft is straight and strong. Whorls come in many shapes and sizes, from tiny clay beads to large disks of wood, metal, or even CDs. Spindles can be rustic and plain or elegant and exotic. Spindles that weigh only a few grams are designed for spinning the finest laceweight yarn, while heavier ones produce strong, bulky yarn. Spindles fall into two groups: supported and suspended.

Supported Spindles
A supported spindle rests on a surface while it is being turned. A Navajo spindle rests on the ground, while a tahkli or Russian lace spindle may spin on a table or in a small dish. Because these spindles are spun on a surface, they don't bear any weight, so a very soft or a very fine yarn can be spun on them. Almost all supported spindles have the whorl near the bottom of the spindle shaft.

Suspended or Drop Spindles
Drop spindles are suspended from the fiber source and turn freely in the air. A top-whorl or high-whorl spindle has the whorl close to the top of the shaft and is usually topped with a hook. Bottom-whorl or low-whorl spindles have the whorl near the base of the spindle and may have a hook at the top, a groove near the top of the shaft, or nothing at all to secure the yarn. (Some spindles can be used as either a top-whorl or a bottom-whorl.) Mid-whorl spindles have the whorl farther from the top than a top-whorl, but they are used as top-whorls. A Turkish spindle looks like a bottom-whorl spindle without the whorl—near the bottom a removable crosspiece of wood serves as both a whorl and a winding tool. As the spinner creates yarn, she wraps it around the crossed "arms"; when the spindle is full, she removes the crosspiece from the shaft, takes the arms apart, and is left with a ball of yarn ready to use.

This Navajo spindle, more than three feet long, rests on the ground while the spinner turns it.

Tahkli spindles are 6–8 inches long, commonly made of metal, that are used to spin cotton and other fine fibers.

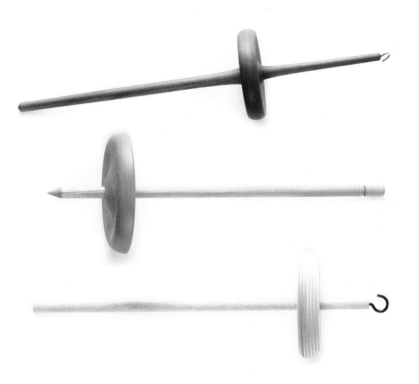

A mid-whorl spindle, bottom-whorl spindle, and top-whorl spindle.

The arms on a Turkish spindle are removable.

CHOOSING YOUR FIRST SPINDLE

There are many beautiful lightweight spindles available, but you may want to practice drafting before trying one of these. Lightweight spindles are designed to spin thin yarn. Your first spindle should weigh between two and three ounces (56 and 84 grams), heavy enough to continue to turn while you learn to draft out the fibers. If you choose one that is too heavy, you will quickly learn why they are called drop spindles. A well-balanced spindle is a delight, so check to see how well it spins before purchasing it—tie some yarn on the spindle and give it a twist. The spindle should turn smoothly without much wobbling and continue to spin for some time.

Your first spindle should weigh between two and three ounces, heavy enough to continue to turn while you learn to draft out the fibers.

Top Whorl

1. Tie the leader to the shaft below the whorl.

2. Catch the leader with the hook.

SET UP YOUR SPINDLE: ATTACHING THE LEADER

Once you have chosen your spindle, take a piece of plied wool yarn about 18 inches (46 cm) long (called a **leader**) and tie it onto the spindle shaft; any knot will do. If you have a top-whorl spindle, tie the leader underneath the whorl, bring the leader up and over the whorl, and catch it with the hook. If there is a little notch in the whorl, place your leader in the notch. You can wrap the yarn around the hook once for security if you like.

For a bottom-whorl spindle, tie the leader above the whorl, and then spiral the yarn up the spindle shaft. Some spinners tie the leader above the whorl, then bring the yarn down under the whorl, around the bottom of the shaft, then back up to the top. Both ways work—see which one you like best. If there is a hook at the top of the shaft, catch the yarn with it and you are ready to go.

If your spindle has a groove in the shaft or a smooth spindle top, you will need to make a half hitch knot to hold the yarn on the spindle. To make a half hitch, wrap the leader around your index finger with the tail end of the yarn underneath. Slip the spindle shaft into the loop around your finger, then gently slide your finger out. Pull the tail end of the yarn up and tighten the loop around the spindle shaft.

GET TO KNOW YOUR SPINDLE

Once the leader is on, play with the spindle. Remember, most yarns are spun clockwise (to the right), so practice rolling or twisting the shaft to spin in that direction. Most spinners hold their fiber in the left hand and the spindle in their right hand, but try both hands and see which feels more comfortable to you. The hand you hold the leader in will be your fiber hand; the hand you use to twist the spindle will be your twist hand. Hold the leader in your fiber hand and use your twist hand to give the spindle a twist to the right. Practice until you can get the spindle to turn smoothly. (You will have to stop and let the leader unwind periodically so you don't accumulate too much twist.)

BEGIN TO SPIN!

Once you are comfortable with the twisting action that makes the spindle spin, it is time to add some wool. Take a rolag or some

Bottom Whorl

1. Tie the leader above the whorl.

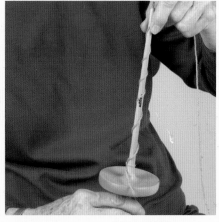

2. Spiral the leader up the shaft.

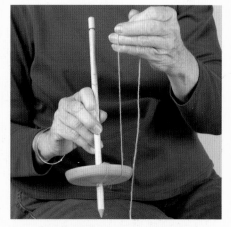

3. You may prefer to wrap the leader around the shaft under the whorl.

4. Wrap the leader around your finger to begin a half hitch.

5. Slip the shaft into the loop.

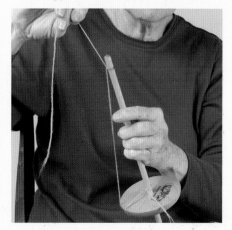

6. Pull the tail up to tighten the half hitch.

Once the leader is on, play with the spindle.

Remember, most yarns are spun clockwise (to the right), so practice

rolling or twisting the shaft to spin in that direction.

Pinching the yarn keeps the twist out of the drafting triangle so you can draft. It also gives you something to draft against.

carded roving and pre-draft it a little to start the fibers moving past one another more easily (see page 14). After pre-drafting, you may want to wrap this fiber around your wrist so it won't get caught in your yarn as you spin.

Join Fiber and Leader

Fluff out the end of the leader. With your fiber hand, pinch the pre-drafted fiber and the leader together between your thumb and index finger. With the twist hand, spin the spindle clockwise and watch as the twist runs up the leader and grabs the fibers in your hand. After the twist has joined the fiber and the leader, give a gentle tug with your twist hand to test the join.

Add Twist

After you have made the join, twist the spindle again, allowing a little twist to run up the leader, then drop the spindle in your lap before it begins to spin backward. This method of adding twist and adding fibers in two steps is commonly called **park and draft**. Slide your twisting hand above the spindle, pinch the leader, and gently draft out some fibers. Pinching the yarn keeps the twist out of the drafting triangle so you can draft. It also gives you something to draft against. The twisting/pinching hand keeps the twist under control while the fiber hand drafts out the fibers. Once the yarn is formed, open the pinching/twist hand and let the twist run up to stabilize the fibers you have just drafted.

SPIN, WIND, JOIN

Continue to twist the spindle, stop it in your lap, pinch and draft. Remember that to draft the fiber, you have to feel the fibers slip past one another. You determine the size of the yarn by how much you pull the fibers out. A few fibers make a fine yarn; many fibers make a bulkier yarn. If too much twist gets into your fiber, slide your fiber hand back a little to allow more room for the twist and then draft out those fibers.

When your yarn seems longer than your arms, it's time to wind it onto the spindle. Keeping the yarn taut, unhook the yarn from the spindle or undo the half hitch and wind the yarn on the spindle clockwise to make a cone, under the whorl on a top-whorl spindle

Join Leader and Begin to Spin

1. Fluff out the end of the leader.

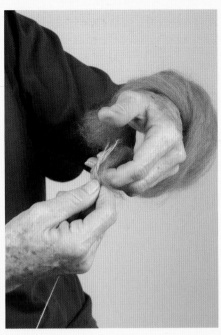

2. Hold the leader and fiber together.

3. Allow twist to run up the leader and grab the fibers to join them.

4. Stop the spindle in your lap before it begins to twist backward.

5. Pinch the leader and draft out more fiber.

6. Pinching the yarn keeps twist out of the drafting triangle.

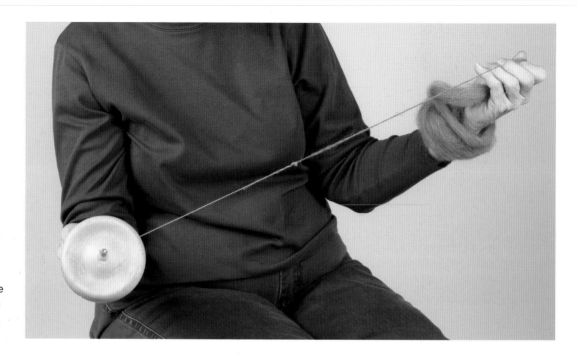

Wind On: Unhook the yarn from the spindle and wind it clockwise onto the shaft.

and above on a bottom-whorl. The neater the yarn is wound onto the spindle, the easier it will be to take it off the spindle later.

When you run out of fiber, add some more by fluffing out the end of the yarn you are spinning and overlapping it with new fiber just like you did with the fiber and leader. When you are comfortable working with pre-drafted fiber, try some fiber that hasn't been pre-drafted.

TAKE IT OUT OF PARK: SUSPENDING THE SPINDLE

Once you feel comfortable spinning the spindle and stopping it on your lap, try to spin with the spindle suspended. Stand up and continue to draft the fibers out the same way, but instead of stopping your spindle let it spin. When the spindle stops turning clockwise and starts going backwards, add more clockwise twist. If the spindle starts to turn in the opposite direction, the twist will come out of your yarn and turn it back into fluff. The fluff isn't strong enough to support the weight of the spindle, which will fall to the floor (a reminder of why this is called a "drop spindle"). Using a top whorl spindle allows you to add twist by rolling the spindle on your thigh. To add clockwise twist with your right hand, roll the spindle up your thigh; with your left hand, roll the spindle down your thigh.

If the spindle starts to turn in the opposite direction, the twist will come out of your yarn and turn it back into fluff.

Stand Up: Stand up to practice drafting and adding twist at the same time.

Spin Faster: Many spinners turn the spindle by rolling it between their palm and outer thigh.

Wind Off: Use a shoebox to hold the spindle while you wind the yarn into a ball.

You'll probably find that spinning a little every day is more helpful in getting the hang of it than trying to learn in one intensive sitting. It will take some time for all the elements to come together, but soon you will be spinning like a champ.

MANAGING YOUR SPUN YARN

Sooner or later you will have more yarn on your spindle than you can manage comfortably. If you want to use the yarn as a single strand, wind the yarn off the spindle and make a skein or a ball. You can use a shoe box with holes punched in it to hold your spindle. To make a skein, wrap the yarn around your elbow, a chair with a straight back, or a niddy-noddy (see page 66). Before you use your yarn, you will want to set the twist (see page 68). If you are going to ply your yarn (see page 54), wind it into a ball and then spin another spindle full.

CHAPTER FOUR

Spinning Wheels 101

While some spinners are completely satisfied with the spindle's beauty and portability, the speed and flexibility of the spinning wheel can't be beat. Practicing a bit on a spindle before learning to use a spinning wheel will give your hands some experience drafting out fibers before you sit down at the wheel.

Upright wheel

WHEEL HISTORY

The earliest spinning wheels were spindle wheels, like the charka or great wheel. Spinners turned the wheel with one hand and drafted out the fibers with the other. After the yarn was formed, the spinner would change hand positions to allow the yarn to wind onto the spindle. The spindle was a long, thin, tapered piece; yarn was made at the point of the spindle and wound onto its shaft. (Remember the story of *Sleeping Beauty*? She pricked her finger on a spindle.) Spinning with this kind of wheel required two separate motions.

The invention of the flyer wheel changed all that, allowing the spinner to make yarn and wind it onto a bobbin without changing hand positions. With the incorporation of the **treadle** (foot pedal), the spinner could add twist with her feet, make yarn with her hands, and allow the wheel to wind the yarn onto the bobbin. Over time, spinning wheels have been refined to meet a variety of spinning needs.

VARIATIONS ON THE WHEEL

Although you know the basic parts of the spinning wheel, they may be difficult to find or identify on wheels from different manufacturers (and even different centuries).

Wheel Style
The wheel pictured on page 29 is in the Saxony style, where the flyer assembly is to the side of the drive wheel. This is what most people think of when they picture a spinning wheel. The other popular style is called an upright wheel, where the flyer sits above the drive wheel and the treadle below.

Drive and Tensioning
The flyer and bobbin allow the yarn to be wound on the wheel without the spinner having to change position. To make the yarn fill the bobbin, the bobbin and the flyer have to move at different speeds during the winding-on process. There are three ways this happens:

Flyer-lead or scotch tension: The drive band is on the flyer, and there is a brake band on the bobbin. When the bobbin slows down,

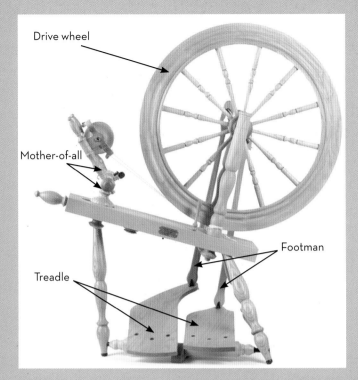

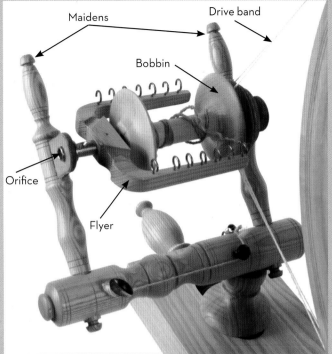

Parts of the Wheel

The wheel pictured here is traditional in design.
Most of its parts are also found on other wheels, although they may look very different.

Treadle: Where the action starts. Depending on the wheel, there can be one or two (as shown here).

Footman: Connects the treadle to the drive wheel. Each time you push the treadle, the drive wheel turns.

Drive wheel: The big wheel that concentrates the power of the treadle. The drive wheel is connected to the flyer by the drive band.

Drive band: The continuous band that transfers the action from the drive wheel to the flyer. (In the case of a double drive wheel, it also drives the bobbin; see page 31.)

Flyer: The U-shaped piece with a metal shaft in the middle to hold the bobbin. The arms of the flyer usually have hooks to allow the yarn to wind onto the bobbin evenly. The hooks may all be on the top, or they may be on the top of one arm and the bottom of the other. Instead of hooks, some wheels have a yarn guide on one side of the flyer that you move up and down to fill the bobbin evenly.

Orifice: The opening located at the bottom of the U of the flyer. Yarn passes through the orifice and is wound onto the bobbin.

Bobbin: The spool that stores the yarn after it has been spun. It rests on the metal shaft in the center of the flyer and should turn freely on the shaft.

Maidens: The upright arms that hold the flyer and the bobbin in place. One of these pieces usually turns so the flyer can be removed and the bobbins changed.

Mother-of-all: The base and maidens that supports the flyer.

Types of Wheels

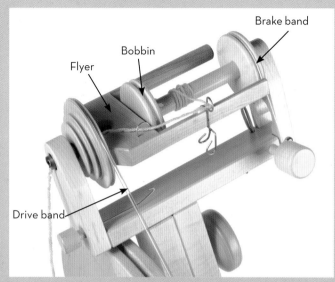

Flyer-lead or scotch tension

Brake band · Bobbin · Flyer · Drive band

Bobbin-lead

Flyer · Brake band · Bobbin · Drive band

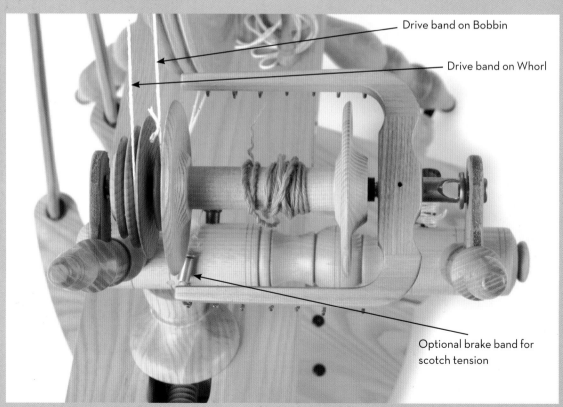

Drive band on Bobbin

Drive band on Whorl

Optional brake band for scotch tension

Double-drive

the yarn winds on. Ashford Joy, Lendrum, and Majacraft are some of the wheels that use scotch tension.

Bobbin-lead or irish or Indian-head tension: The drive band is on the bobbin and the brake band is on the flyer. On this wheel, the flyer slows down and the bobbin continues to turn to wind the yarn on. Most Louet wheels use this method.

Double-drive: The drive band is one long band folded over, with one part going around the flyer whorl and the other part around the bobbin whorl. Because the bobbin whorl is smaller than the flyer whorl, the bobbin turns faster than the flyer and pulls the yarn on. The Ashford Elizabeth is a double-drive wheel. Many wheels have the ability to be either single-drive or double-drive. Schacht, Jensen, and Ashford all make wheels that can be either scotch tension or double-drive.

Clockwise from top left, a bobbin with the whorl incorporated (for a bobbin-lead wheel), a flyer with the whorl incorporated (for a scotch tension wheel), and a selection of whorls (for a scotch tension or double-drive wheel).

Bobbins and Whorls

Double-drive and scotch tension wheels have a whorl or pulley on the flyer that holds the drive band. Some wheels, such as the Ashford traditional single-drive, have the whorl on the flyer close to the orifice, while other wheels like the Schacht or Ashford Elizabeth have a removable whorl at the end of the spindle shaft. This whorl has to lock onto the spindle with a screw mechanism or shaped shaft so they act as one unit. Wheels that can be either double-drive or scotch tension often come with bobbins whose ends are different. To use the wheel in a double-drive setup, place the drive band on the smaller end of the bobbin. To spin with scotch tension, place the brake band on the larger end of the bobbin.

On a bobbin-lead wheel, where the drive band sits directly on the bobbin, the whorl is located on the bobbin.

Place the drive band in the smaller (top) groove for double drive and in the larger (bottom) groove for scotch tension.

Drive-Wheel Ratios

The drive-wheel ratio is related to the diameters of the drive wheel and the whorl. Drive-wheel ratios are often written as 7:1 or 12.5:1. These numbers refer to how many times the flyer or bobbin goes around for every complete rotation of the drive wheel. In the first example, the flyer or bobbin turns seven times as the drive wheel

Choosing a wheel is as important as choosing a car. Just as you would test-drive a car, sit down and test several wheels before you make a choice.

revolves once. The higher the drive-wheel ratio, the more twist that goes into your yarn. Most beginning spinners find it easier to spin with a ratio in the range of 6:1 to 9:1, rather than with a higher one that adds more twist. Most modern wheels have a choice of at least three drive-wheel ratios, so you can use a different whorl to adjust your wheel instead of your spinning.

CHOOSING A WHEEL

Choosing a wheel is as important as choosing a car. In fact, my wheel has outlived a couple of cars. Just as you would test-drive a car, sit down and test several wheels before you make a choice. If you're not ready to buy a wheel, you can borrow or rent one to try it out first. Ask your local spinning shop, handspinners or handweavers guild, or a friend who spins if she knows of any wheels available to try.

Modern wheels can make a wide variety of yarns, but one may be more suited for a certain type of yarn. In general, a bobbin-lead wheel is better at making bulky yarns, while a flyer-lead wheel makes a fine laceweight yarn with more ease. I often ask knitters about their favorite needle sizes to help them decide which wheel to try first. Someone who loves to knit on size 15 needles most of the time may be happier with a Louet, and a lace knitter will be more satisfied with a double-drive or scotch tension wheel.

§ How does it feel to your feet and legs? You want a wheel that treadles easily. Spend some time just treadling and pay attention to how your legs and ankles feel. Treadling action can be quite different between various wheels, so look for one that fits your body.

§ Do you want a single-treadle or a double-treadle? Many people find it easier to keep the wheel turning using two feet instead of one. Try both and see which one feels most comfortable. Using both feet may also be easier on your body. My single-treadle wheel has one large treadle that both feet push at the same time.

§ How many different weights of yarn will you want to make? Choose a wheel with at least three drive-wheel ratios. This will allow you to make different sizes of yarn with ease.

§ What is your fidget tolerance level when it comes to changing bobbins and adjusting drive bands? Some wheels are simpler to adjust than others, but they may not be as sensitive to the small adjustments you might want to make. Decide what is most important to you.

§ Will your wheel travel with you? My first wheel was an Ashford Traditional and I drove a VW bug. It was always amusing to watch me load and unload my wheel. If you plan to take your wheel long distances, you might consider a folding wheel.

§ How easy is it to get parts? You will need at least three bobbins to start with, but a few extra bobbins always come in handy. (You could get by with only one bobbin and use storage bobbins or balls of yarn when you ply, but the bother of constantly emptying bobbins will quickly drive you mad.) If your impish cousin breaks the mother-of-all or your dog chews through the footman, will you be able to get service easily?

The most important thing to look for in a wheel is totally subjective. *Do you love it?* Hopefully, you are starting a long-term relationship with your wheel. Your wheel should make you smile and feel good when you sit down to spin.

CHAPTER FIVE

Getting Acquainted with Your Wheel

Take some time to make friends with your wheel before you start to spin. Set aside time when you won't be interrupted, put on some good music, and take a good look at your wheel. Figure out where the drive band and the brake band go. Learn how to take off the flyer and change the bobbins. If you don't have an instruction book, check the manufacturer's website or ask the shop where you bought your wheel.

Change Bobbins

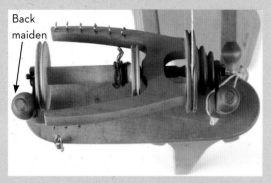

To release the flyer on this Ashford Traditional, you can rotate the back maiden or pop the flyer shaft out of the back bearing.

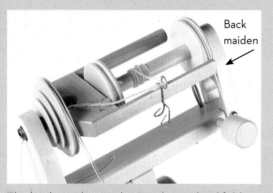

The back maiden on this Lendrum wheel folds down to release the flyer.

The flyer of this Majacraft wheel is designed in two parts; the orifice and arms are unscrewed from the shaft to change the bobbin.

CHANGING BOBBINS AND WHORLS

Most wheels have a maiden that folds down or rotates so you can remove the flyer; some wheels have no front maiden and the end of the flyer shaft is threaded so it screws into the back maiden or upright. It will be easier to take off the flyer and bobbin if you take off the drive band and/or brake band before removing the flyer. Some scotch tension flyers have the whorl built in at the front of the flyer and others have a separate whorl that screws onto or fits the end of the spindle shaft. If you have a whorl that screws on, screw it on carefully—you don't want to strip the threaded area. Some whorls screw on clockwise and some counterclockwise. If your wheel can function as scotch tension or double drive make sure you have the bobbin on the correct way (see page 31). After you have put your wheel back together, it is time to get to work.

PRACTICE TREADLING

Most yarn is spun clockwise (to the right), so start your wheel in that direction and just treadle. It isn't a race; treadle slowly but with enough momentum that the wheel continues to turn clockwise and doesn't stall and go backward.

Think of the drive wheel as a clock. If you position the footman (the part of the wheel that connects the treadle to the drive wheel) at 1:00 and make the first treadle strong, momentum will help keep the wheel going clockwise. Take off your shoes—your bare foot is more flexible and it may be easier to treadle. (It will also protect the finish on your treadle.) You may find it easier to use your hand to start the wheel, but be careful not to knock off the drive band when you do.

While you practice, sit on different chairs to find which one is the most comfortable. Both chair height and seat depth can make a big difference in treadling comfort. My favorite spinning chair is an inexpensive secretary's chair from an office supply store. It has a small amount of back support and no arms, and I can adjust the padded seat to the perfect height. However, the wheels on a chair can be tricky on a smooth floor, so always spin on a rug. Treadle while you talk on the phone or read until it becomes a natural movement.

Practice Treadling: Practice while you read or watch television.

Prepare to Treadle: Position the wheel with the footman at 1:00.

ADJUSTING TENSION

Learning how to adjust the tension on your wheel is crucial to learning how to spin. You want to work in partnership with your wheel, and if you have the drive band and the tension (brake band) adjusted properly, it will be easy.

Scotch tension wheels usually have a brake band with a spring or a rubber band to control tension. The brake band goes over the bobbin and is controlled with a knob. To tighten the tension, turn the knob so the spring or rubber band is stretched out a little. The more

> The tighter the tension, the harder the wheel will be to treadle and the faster the yarn will be pulled onto the bobbin.

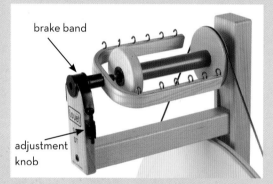

Adjust Tension

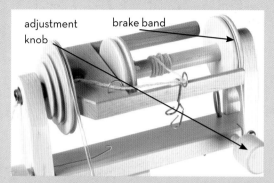

Brake band and adjustment knob on scotch tension wheel

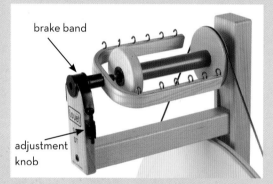

Brake band and adjustment knob on bobbin-lead wheel

On a double-drive wheel, a screw mechanism adjusts the tension on the flyer and bobbin.

the spring or rubber band is stretched out, the stronger the wheel will pull the yarn onto the bobbin. Relax the tension, and the yarn will pull on more slowly.

On bobbin-lead wheels like the Louet, the drive band is on the bobbin and the brake is a strap over the flyer. Again, the tighter the tension on the brake band the stronger the pull of the wheel. If the yarn is being pulled on too fast, loosen the brake band over the flyer.

On a double-drive wheel, you have only one adjustment because the drive band controls both the flyer and the bobbin. Usually there is a screw-type mechanism that tightens the tension on the drive band by moving the flyer farther away from the wheel. When you tighten the drive band, the yarn will be pulled on more firmly. However, if the drive band tension is too tight, it will be hard to keep the wheel going in the same direction. Loosen the tension on the drive band, and the yarn will be pulled onto the wheel gently.

ADJUSTING THE DRIVE BAND

Drive bands are usually made out of cotton string or polyurethane. Drive bands made out of cotton can be adjusted; the polyurethane bands are self-adjusting. There should be just enough tension on the drive-band so that when the wheel is treadled, the wheel will turn the flyer or bobbin easily without any drive-band slippage. If the drive band is too loose, increase the tension just so the drive band doesn't slip. If the drive band is too tight, the wheel will be hard to treadle. When adjusting the tension on your drive band, loosen it enough that when you treadle the flyer doesn't move. Then tighten the tension gradually until the flyer turns when the drive wheel does.

Most wheels adjust the drive band by changing the distance between the flyer and the drive wheel. The mother-of-all is often attached to a screw mechanism or hinge to move it closer or farther away from the drive wheel. Look at the wheel manufacturer's information to see how to adjust the tension on the drive band.

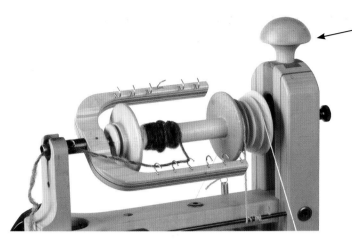

Adjust the drive band: Turn the screw to move the flyer closer to or farther from the drive wheel.

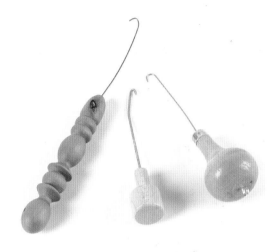

A selection of orifice hooks

GETTING READY TO SPIN

To start, you will want to be on the largest whorl for the slowest speed. Remember: *slow is bigger*. The largest whorl will give you the most control.

The yarn will be wound onto your bobbin with the help of a **leader**, a piece of wool yarn tied to the bobbin. Start with a piece of plied wool yarn about 24 inches (61 cm) long. You want the leader to wind onto the bobbin and not slip, so tie the yarn on firmly. Leave a long enough tail to wrap around the bobbin again and tie another knot and then a third knot. Once the leader is on your bobbin, take the yarn over the hooks of the flyer. It doesn't matter which hook you start on, but it is important that the yarn is engaged by all the other hooks between that one and the orifice. Some wheels don't have hooks but have a thread guide that moves up and down the flyer arm; be sure to thread your leader through that guide and then the one near the orifice.

To get the leader through the orifice, you will probably need a small tool called an **orifice hook**, which you insert into the orifice to catch the yarn and pull it through. Some wheels have built-in orifice hooks and holders; if yours doesn't, tie a string around the hook handle and hang it nearby. Keep the orifice hook close at hand, because you will need it frequently. The orifice of some wheels will be large enough that you can just pull the leader through with your finger, while Majacraft wheels have been designed without an orifice at all.

Attach the Leader

1. Tie the leader firmly on the bobbin.

2. Wrap the yarn around the bobbin again and tie two more knots.

3. Pass the leader through the hooks, if your flyer has them.

Orifices

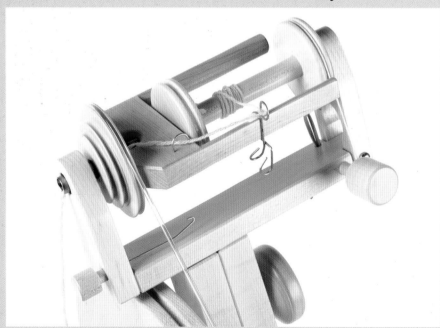

If your flyer has a sliding guide, pass the yarn through it, then through the orifice.

With a Majacraft "delta" orifice, pass the yarn through the triangle.

TENSION IN ACTION

By now you understand the theory of how the brake or tension works on your wheel (see page 37.) Spend some time playing with the tension now that you have a leader on the bobbin. Remember the tighter the brake band, the faster the yarn will be pulled onto the bobbin and the harder it will be to treadle.

Start with very light or no tension on your brake band, so that your bobbin spins with no drag. Hold onto your leader and start treadling. The leader should pull onto the bobbin very slowly or not at all while the leader gets more and more twisted. Now tighten the tension on the brake band a lot and see what a difference it makes. The leader will feel like it is being sucked right out of your hand. Pull the leader back out of the orifice and keep adjusting the tension on your brake band, degree by degree. (You may need to stop and let the twist run out of the leader or turn the wheel backward if the leader gets too twisted and kinked.) Adjust the tension in small increments; an eighth or a quarter turn of the tension knob changes the tension considerably.

If you have a double-drive wheel, do this same exercise but adjust the drive band, not the brake band. Tighten and loosen the tension in small increments and see how it changes the rate at which the leader is pulled onto the bobbin.

Learning how to adjust the tension on your wheel makes all the difference when it comes to an enjoyable and productive spinning experience. The looser the drive band and the brake bands are, the easier it will be to treadle, but if they are too loose the yarn won't draw in. Don't be afraid to play with your wheel and find the perfect tension for the yarn you are spinning. Be aware however, that each fiber or size of yarn may require different tension.

Trust me—learning how to adjust your spinning wheel is way easier than using a computer. Start with the tension very loose, with no draw-in, and tighten the brake or drive band (for double-drive) until the yarn is pulled on firmly when you relax your hold on it. As you are spinning you may make small adjustments; an eighth or a quarter turn is all you need. Whenever you begin to spin, a good way to find the perfect tension is to loosen the tension so there is no draw-in at all and then gently tighten the tension until it is comfortable. As I tell my students, "Loose till tight until it's right!"

NONSLIP LEADERS

Judith MacKenzie McCuin makes a lark's head knot on a bight for her leaders, and they never slip. Take about a yard of plied wool yarn and fold it in half. Hold the doubled yarn under the bobbin and then bring the tails through the loop on top. Pull tight on the loose ends to snug up the lark's head. Fold the yarn in half again, bring the tails through the loop, and tighten it again to make the bight.

 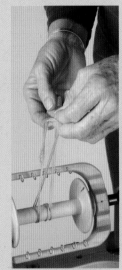

1. Pass the tails through the loop for a lark's head knot.

2. Bring the tails through the second loop to make the bight.

CHAPTER SIX

Spinning Yarn on a Wheel

When you're comfortable with treadling your wheel and adjusting the tension, you're ready to start making yarn! You'll notice that the basic elements—adding twist, drafting out fiber—are the same as for spinning on a drop spindle.

Spinning on a wheel may feel complicated and awkward at first. It takes some time and practice to feel natural. While you're learning, keep repeating the sequence: Pinch, draw back, relax, wind on.

EASY AS ONE, TWO, THREE: START TO SPIN ON THE WHEEL

Start with some of the carded fiber you pre-drafted (see page 14). Fluff out the end of your leader with your fingers, place the leader on the fiber, and hold them together with the thumb and index finger of your back hand or fiber hand. Slowly treadle clockwise and watch the twist come up the leader and grab the fibers in your hand. After the twist has built up a little bit, use your other hand (the front hand or twist hand) to pinch the leader below the join to control the twist. Now gently draft the fibers out by pulling backward with your fiber hand. When you open your front hand, the twist will run up, grab the loose fibers, and turn them into yarn. *Relax your back hand and give the yarn to the wheel.* Just as on a spindle, the yarn is created in the drafting triangle.

Now start the spinning process over again. The front hand controls the twist by pinching, and the back hand drafts the fiber out. You determine the size of the yarn by how much fiber you draft out; a few fibers make a fine yarn, while many fibers add bulk.

Spinning on a wheel may feel complicated and awkward at first. It takes some time and practice to feel natural. While you're learning, keep repeating the sequence: Pinch, draw back, relax, wind on.

You are stronger than the wheel, so you must *remember to relax your back hand and let the yarn wind onto the wheel.* If you don't, too much twist will accumulate and the yarn won't wind on. Tighten the tension a little if necessary to pull the yarn onto the wheel.

SHORT FORWARD DRAW

If you are getting frustrated with too much twist (or very uneven twist) as you draft backward, try another drafting method. Instead of drafting backward with your fiber hand, pull the fiber toward the wheel with your twist hand: Pinch down a little with your twist hand and feed the yarn to the wheel. Then relax your twist hand and move it back to where it started and pull forward another section of fiber. Pull forward, move back. This drafting technique gets the yarn onto the bobbin faster and doesn't allow as much twist to build up.

| **Start to Spin the Wheel** | **Practice, Practice, Practice** |

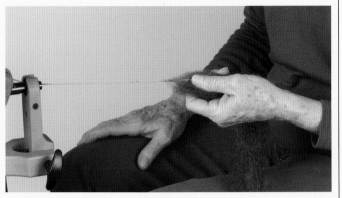

1. Hold the leader and fiber together.

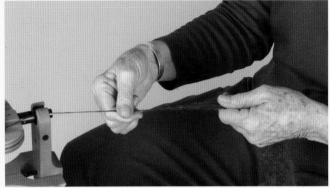

1. Pinch with the front hand to control the twist.

2. Pinch the leader in front of the twist.

2. Draft the fibers out with the back hand.

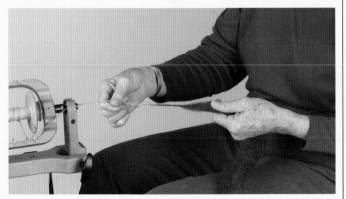

3. Pull back with your fiber hand to begin drafting.

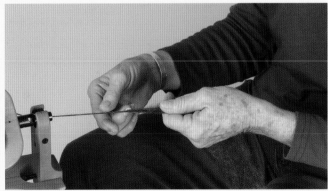

3. Release the pinch, watch the twist run up, and let the yarn wind on.

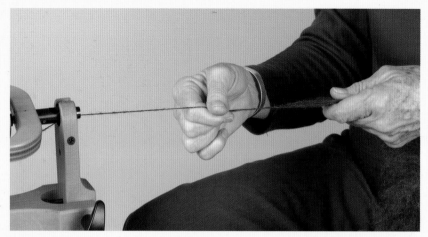

1. Pinch the yarn with your twist hand.

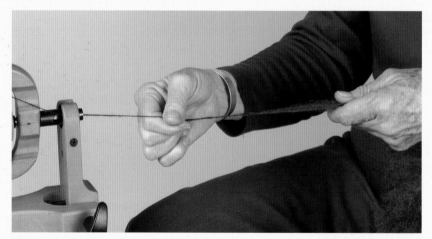

2. Pull the yarn forward with your twist hand.

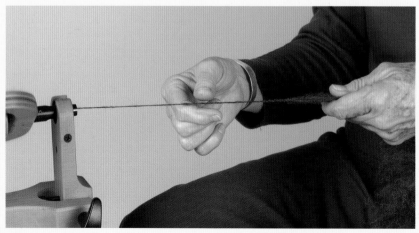

3. Release the pinch, move the twist hand back, and pinch again.

MORE OF A GOOD THING: ADDING MORE FIBER

Soon you will run out of fiber and have to make a join. This is very much like joining the leader to the fiber when you began to spin, but it requires a little more care to make a strong, smooth join that won't leave a lump or fray when it is rubbed. With a little practice, though, you'll be able to make joins that don't show at all.

When you are coming to the end of your fiber source, don't spin to the absolute end before you make a join—you need a little unspun fiber on the end to merge with your new batch. Leave almost a full staple length of your fiber and fluff out the ends. Pinch your old and new fiber together with the thumb and index finger of your fiber hand, treadle to let some twist run into the fibers, then gently draft the old and new fibers together. If you have drafted the fibers well, there shouldn't be a lump, and you should be able to run your fingers over the join and not disturb the fibers. Don't just wrap the new fibers around the old ones—they need to be drafted together for strength.

If your yarn has broken, leaving a skinny, tightly twisted end, you probably won't be able to fluff the ends enough to make a strong join. Instead look farther along the yarn, maybe even on the bobbin, to find a fatter and less twisted area in your yarn. Break the yarn there, fluff out the fibers, and then make a join. Take some time to just practice making joins and then testing them for strength.

MOVE THE YARN TO FILL THE BOBBIN

Each time you start a new rolag or handful of fiber, move your yarn to a different hook on your flyer or move the sliding yarn guide. You want the yarn to fill the bobbin evenly without any great hills or valleys of yarn. Repeat this process over and over again until the bobbin is full. If you have a buildup in one area of the bobbin, it can avalanche and the old yarn can cover your newer yarn. This becomes a problem when it is time to take the yarn off the bobbin.

As your bobbin fills, you may notice the yarn is not winding on as easily as it was at the beginning. Adjust this by tightening the tension on the brake band (or drive band if you have a double-drive wheel)—just an eighth of a turn is usually enough.

Adding Fiber

1. Hold the fluffed-out end of your yarn in the new fiber.

2. Let the twist run up from the old yarn into the new fiber.

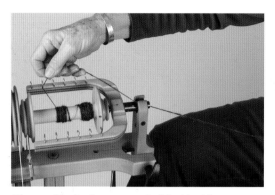

Change hooks for an evenly filled bobbin.

At left, an evenly filled bobbin; at right, an uneven bobbin that may be difficult to use.

CHECK YOUR WORK

Stop spinning occasionally and check your yarn for strength. Before you let a section of yarn wind onto the bobbin, hold onto the strand with both hands and give it a gentle tug to see whether it has enough twist. If there isn't enough twist, you will feel the fibers slipping between your hands. If the fibers start slipping or drifting, treadle a couple of times to add more twist before you let the yarn wind onto the bobbin.

When you are satisfied that your yarn is strong enough, take a length of yarn in one hand and let it twist back on itself to see how it would look as a balanced plied yarn. If it looks a little loose and open, you need more twist. If it has so many corkscrews they won't relax, you need less twist. Testing your yarn to see how it would look as a balanced ply can only be done with freshly spun yarn; if the yarn is more than 15 minutes old it won't give you an accurate sample.

TWIST, MORE OR LESS

How much twist do you need? It depends! What is your yarn going to be used for? If you are making long-wearing yarn for socks or mittens, you might want more twist than for a soft hat. A warp yarn for a rug would need lots of twist to be durable. You need enough twist to keep the yarn from drifting as a singles, but too much twist in a singles can cause it to skew and your knitted square will turn into a trapezoid. Too much twist looks like little corkscrews or pigtails that won't relax when you try to straighten them out. If you have a lot of overtwist, the corkscrews wrap around the hooks on the flyer and won't let the yarn wind on, preventing you from continuing to spin. Check the section on Troubleshooting on page 52 for hints. Keep in mind that if you are going to ply your yarn (see page 54), it needs enough twist to hold together during plying.

Test Your Yarn

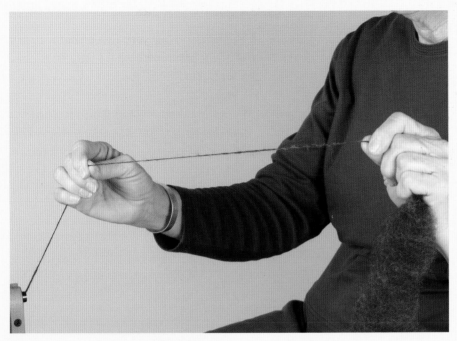

1. Test your yarn for strength.

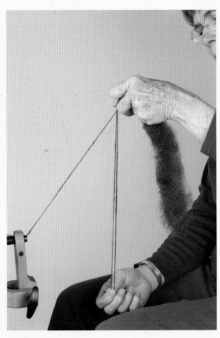

2. Let a length of yarn twist back on itself.

3. This length of yarn is too loose and underspun.

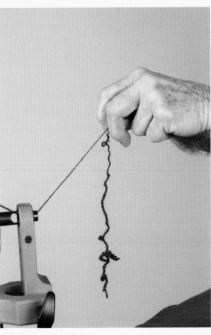

4. This length of yarn is too kinked and overspun.

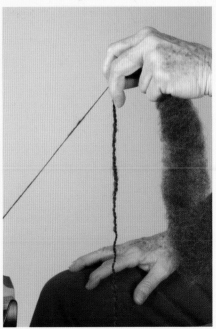

5. Not too tight, not too loose, just right.

TIPS FOR HAPPIER SPINNING

Spinning has a lot more to do with finesse than with brute strength. You can make amazing yarn if you just relax and let the fibers flow. (Could this be the Zen of spinning?)

§ *Sit up straight.* Remember to breathe and maintain good posture—just because the yarn disappears into the orifice doesn't mean you have to, too. If you hold your hands closer to your body than to the wheel, you will have more time to see your yarn before it disappears onto the bobbin. In addition to making a more consistent yarn, it is so much better for your body.

§ *Watch where you pinch.* As you draft, remember to pinch where the yarn has already been formed, slightly in front of the drafting triangle. If you pinch right where the twist grabs the fibers, you will make a slub. (In fact, if you wanted to make a slub yarn, this is just how you would go about it.)

§ *Keep a tidy drafting triangle.* Pay attention to the fibers in the drafting triangle. As the twist grabs the front ends of the fibers, the tail ends of those fibers should be under the control of the fiber hand. Stop spinning and reorganize any fibers that try to escape or slide past your fiber hand; you want all the fibers under slight tension as the twist runs up.

§ *Allow just enough twist.* If too much twist enters the drafting triangle, the fibers can be hard to draft. You can slide your fiber hand back slightly to allow the fibers to move again. Another trick is to temporarily make the twist move backward or untwist. Use your front hand to pinch the fibers directly in front of the drafting triangle and then roll them counterclockwise with your thumb and forefinger. The twist takes a step backward, releasing the fibers in the drafting triangle and letting you draft again.

§ *Tame tension.* Understand how your brake system works. Start with a loose tension on your wheel and then slowly tighten the brake until it is easy to spin the yarn of your choice. Make small adjustments. Remember that a thick yarn requires more tension; you want the yarn to be pulled onto the wheel before too

Spinning has a lot more to do with finesse than with brute strength. You can make amazing yarn if you just relax and let the fibers flow. (Could this be the Zen of spinning?)

much twist builds up. The opposite is true with fine yarns—you want less tension, because you need more twist to strengthen fewer fibers. Just by adjusting the tension on your wheel you can create a variety of yarn sizes without changing whorls.

§ ***Make a detour.*** If, no matter how little tension you have on your wheel, your yarn is still being pulled onto the bobbin before you are ready, you can lace the yarn across the flyer hooks to slow down the winding-on process. Take the yarn that winds onto the bobbin and place it under one hook, then across to the other flyer arm and under a hook, and then into the orifice. If you don't have hooks on the same side of your flyer arms, you can loop the yarn over the other arm in between the hooks. If you have one arm with a thread guide and a smooth arm on the other side of the flyer, just put the yarn over the empty arm. This technique works especially well on bobbin-lead wheels and allows more time for the twist to build up in your yarn before it is wound onto the bobbin.

§ ***Let the whorl work for you.*** Make use of your different drive-wheel ratios. The larger whorls allow less twist into your yarn and the smaller whorls allow more. Smaller whorls are often called fast whorls, but it isn't so much a matter of speed as how much twist is added each time you treadle. You can spin faster with a smaller whorl, but you have to draft more quickly, too.

To slow down the yarn drawing in through the orifice, thread it across the flyer.

Soon your bobbin will be full of yarn. You can use it just as it is, a **singles** yarn (like Brown Sheep Lamb's Pride or Lopi), or spin another bobbin and ply the two together. If you are making a singles yarn, wind the yarn into a skein and set the twist (see page 68). If you want a plied yarn, keep your yarn on the bobbin and spin another bobbin full.

If you feel like you're fighting with your wheel instead of working in partnership with it, keep this in mind ... *It is always the wheel*. Make sure your wheel is clean and oiled (see page 114), and check for the following issues. Your spinning problems are probably due to a little hiccup in the working of the wheel; when you get it straightened out spinning will be much more enjoyable.

If your ...

... yarn won't wind onto the bobbin:

- Remember to *give the yarn to the wheel*. Don't forget that you are stronger than the wheel and that you have to relax your grip on the yarn so it can wind onto the bobbin. If the yarn becomes too twisted, it won't wind on, and you will need to unwind some of the kinks before starting again. You can drop your yarn and let some of the twist run out, or better yet, stop treadling and draft those fibers out a little more to give the twist somewhere to go.

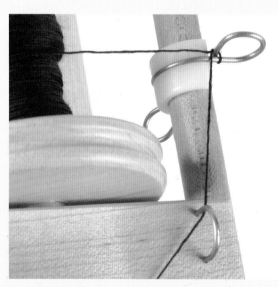

Yarn snagged on a hook or thread guide can bring your spinning to a halt.

- Look at the yarn on the flyer to see whether it has snagged on one of the hooks. Sometimes just a single fiber can stall the whole process.

- Tighten the tension slightly to increase draw-in.

- Make sure the brake band is in the right place, on the bobbin on a scotch tension wheel or on the flyer on a bobbin-lead wheel. If you have a double-drive wheel, make sure one part of the band is on the flyer and one part is on the bobbin.

- If you are using a double-drive wheel, the flyer whorl should be bigger than the bobbin whorl to allow the yarn to wind on. If the whorls are close in size, the draw-in is not very strong. On some wheels, such as the Schacht, the small end of the bobbin is used for double-drive and the large end is for scotch tension. If you get them mixed up, the wheel will not pull the yarn in easily.

- If the leader is not tied tightly enough to the bobbin shaft, it will slip, and you will get lots of twist but no winding on. Put a small piece of tape around the leader to hold it in place or tie on a new leader as shown on page 40.

- Take your flyer off the wheel and check to see that the bobbin rotates freely around the flyer shaft. If it doesn't, clean it out with a cotton swab or rag. If the bobbin is still tight, wrap a little sandpaper around a dowel and use it to clean out the bobbin shaft, or better yet, contact the wheel manufacturer for advice.

- Check to see whether the bobbin ends are loose. If they are, reglue them and let them dry overnight before using.

- See whether any yarn has wrapped around the base of the flyer shaft. This happens when the wheel goes backward for what feels like a nanosecond. When the wheel goes backward, the yarn can fly off the hooks and wrap itself around the front of the flyer. Unwind the yarn with your hand and wrap it back onto the bobbin.

. . . wheel is hard to treadle:

- Loosen the tension a little on your drive band. (Remember, just a small adjustment works best.)

- Loosen the tension on your brake band. (Again, a small adjustment is all you need.)

- If you have maidens that rotate to remove the flyer, make sure they are perfectly parallel when you replace the flyer. If one is slightly askew it is like having another brake. The maidens can also move while you are spinning.

. . . wheel goes backward:

- Start the wheel with the footman in the one o'clock position (see page 37), then make the first treadle firm and strong to develop momentum.

- Loosen the tension on the drive band or brake band just slightly.

. . . yarn is being pulled out of your hands and onto the wheel:

- Loosen the tension on the brake band slightly.

. . . flyer won't turn when the wheel is treadled:

- Increase the tension on the drive band slightly. Most wheels have a way to adjust the tension, generally a screw mechanism that increases the distance between the flyer and the drive wheel. If your band has stretched out too much, you may need to replace it (see page 38). On wheels with self-adjusting drive

bands and no way to increase tension, you may have to buy a new drive band.

. . . yarn is getting too much twist:

- Remember to give the yarn to the wheel.

- Tighten the tension slightly to increase the draw-in.

- If your wheel has several drive-wheel ratios, change to a larger whorl to get less twist per treadle.

- Make sure that your drive band hasn't slipped to a smaller whorl when you weren't looking.

- Try drafting a little faster.

- Try treadling more slowly.

. . . yarn doesn't have enough twist:

- Loosen the tension slightly so the yarn won't pull on so quickly.

- Go to a smaller whorl to get more twist per treadle.

- Draft more slowly to allow more twist to enter the yarn.

- Treadle faster.

Crooked maiden

If your maidens aren't perfectly parallel, they can drag on the flyer.

CHAPTER SEVEN

Plying

You might wonder why anyone in her right mind would ply her yarn. You've just spun 100 yards of yarn, which you are going to twist together to get 50 yards? The most important reason to ply is to create a balanced yarn. A balanced yarn knits up with ease and produces a lovely smooth fabric; the same is true with weaving.

This singles yarn has a lot of Z-twist, which makes a swatch knitted from it bias sharply.

> To ply yarn, you usually take two or more yarns spun in one direction (Z) and twist them together in the opposite direction (S). This action removes a little twist, but it also allows the fibers to relax and regain balance.

WHY PLY?

In a singles yarn, the twist is always trying to escape. You may have experienced this when all of a sudden your knitting yarn just fell apart. It is that sneaky twist. On the other hand, with too much twist you are constantly dealing with kinks and snarls. Too much twist can actually push the piece you are knitting out of shape. Plying can correct this problem. To ply yarn, you usually take two or more yarns spun in one direction (Z) and twist them together in the opposite direction (S). This action removes a little twist, but it also allows the fibers to relax and regain balance.

A plied yarn has several advantages to a singles:

§ A plied yarn is stronger than a singles yarn of the same size.

§ A plied yarn will hold up against abrasion better than a singles yarn will.

§ A plied yarn has a better chance of being uniform. Chances are the skinnier and fatter spots will balance themselves out in a plied yarn.

§ A balanced plied yarn is easier to use than a singles.

§ Most yarns are plied in the opposite direction from the way they were spun, which removes some twist, balances the yarn, and allows the fiber to bloom.

§ A plied yarn has more personality. You can make a yarn with all the plies in the same color or use the barber pole aspect of the yarn to add color and texture.

PREPARE TO PLY

A well-plied yarn starts when you are spinning your singles. There needs to be enough twist in the singles so the yarn won't fall apart when you are plying.

Remember to stop and test the yarn for strength by tugging on it with both hands before you let it wind onto the bobbin or spindle. If there isn't enough twist, loosen your tension or treadle more to add twist before letting the yarn wind on.

When you're spinning, also remember to pull out a length of yarn and let it twist back on itself. That is how your yarn will look as a balanced plied yarn. If it has too little twist, add a little more; if it has too much twist, draft the fibers a little faster. Keep in mind that the more twist in the singles, the more plying twist is needed to make a balanced yarn. When you spin the yarn you like, break off a piece, let it twist back on itself, and keep it as your sample.

PLYING ON A SPINDLE

One of the nicest things about spinning is that there are lots of different ways to accomplish the same goal—including plying on a spindle. You could just use three spindles, spinning yarn on two of them and using the third one to ply directly from the shafts. But unlike spinning wheel bobbins, spindles are often very different from each other on purpose. Not all spinners have more than one spindle that does the same job, which makes it difficult if the yarn you want has two identical plies.

Flowerpot Plying

Rita Buchanan (spinning teacher and author extraordinaire) taught me to ply using a shoebox, two small felt balls, and two clay flowerpots. The flowerpots are an easy way to keep the balls contained and the yarns from tangling.

Poke a hole on each long side of a shoebox and pass the ends of one spindle through the holes to hold it. Wind the yarn from the spindle around one of the balls; repeat with the second spindle and the other ball.

Place each yarn-covered ball under its own upside-down flowerpot. Thread the yarn through the drainage hole of the flowerpot, and you are ready to ply. Tie the two yarns to the leader of the spindle with an overhand knot. Hold the yarns in your fiber hand with a finger between them to keep them from twisting together until you are ready. (You may find it helpful to carry the unplied yarns over your shoulder to keep them from getting tangled in the plying yarn.) Now use your twist hand to turn the spindle *counterclockwise*—the opposite direction from the way it was spun. After the spindle starts turning, slide the twist hand up and pull down lengths of yarn, letting the

One of the nicest things about spinning is that there are lots of different ways to accomplish the same goal.

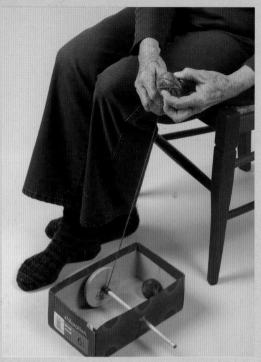

1. Wind yarn from spindle to ball.

2. Place each ball of yarn under its own flower-pot and pass the end of the yarn through the drainage hole.

3. Turn the spindle counterclockwise and let the twist run up into the yarn.

4. Pull out another length of yarns to be plied.

plying twist run into this section. When your yarn has enough twist so that it matches your sample, pull out another length of yarns to be plied. You will have to stop and wind the yarn onto your spindle frequently. When the spindle is full, put it back in the shoe box and wind the yarn into a skein.

PLYING ON A WHEEL

The easiest way to ply on a wheel is to use three bobbins and a *lazy kate* (a bobbin storage device; see right). If you don't have enough bobbins, you can use flowerpots and balls as for plying on a spindle (see page 57).

It's tempting to start plying as soon as you're done spinning—after working hard to make the best singles you possibly can, you may be impatient to see the finished product! But your plying will be much easier and less frustrating if you let the singles "rest" overnight on the bobbins to stabilize the twist.

When you're ready to ply, start with an empty bobbin on your wheel and tie a leader onto the bobbin as you would for spinning. Use a lazy kate to hold your two full bobbins. Put your bobbins on the kate so that they unwind in the same direction, and place the kate on the floor close to your chair. If your kate has a tensioning device, make sure the tension is loose enough to allow the yarn to flow off freely. (The tensioner can be useful to prevent "bobbin backlash"—when the bobbins keep turning with their own momentum.)

PLY COUNTERCLOCKWISE

Holding both yarns together with your leader, tie an overhand knot. *Turn the wheel counterclockwise.* Tighten the brake band a little more than you would for spinning; you want the yarn to wind on smoothly. Your front hand will be busy keeping the twist under control while your back hand stays close to your body and keeps the yarns orderly and ready to ply.

Turn the wheel counterclockwise (in the opposite direction from spinning the singles). Keep the yarns between your hands under light tension, enough to straighten out any kinks in the yarn. As you treadle, move your front hand toward your back hand, bringing the twist down the length of yarn. Make sure the twist stays on the

A KATE BY ANY NAME

A lazy kate is a wonderful tool that should really be called a clever kate because it holds and controls your bobbins while you ply. If you don't have a kate, you can make a simple one with a shoe box and some spare knitting needles.

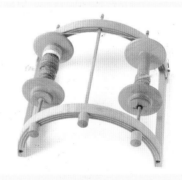

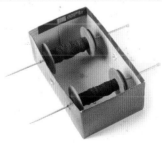

Lazy kates come in a variety of styles; choose one that will fit your bobbins or make one from an old shoebox.

1. Place the kate on the floor close to your chair.

2. Hold the leader and singles together.

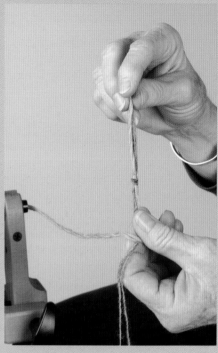

3. Tie the singles and leader in an overhand knot.

orifice side of your front hand; I keep my index finger between the two threads so the twist can't get between my hands. As the twist brings the two yarns together, keep equal tension on both yarns to make sure that they are twisting together, not one wrapping around the other.

Once your front hand meets your back hand, pinch down with your front hand to stop the twist from entering any new yarn, relax, and let the wheel pull the plied yarn onto the bobbin and your front hand toward the orifice. As the plied yarn winds onto the bobbin, a new section of yarn to be plied moves into the area between your hands. Straighten out any kinks in the yarn between your hands and start the process over again. Check the amount of twist against the sample you made while spinning your singles (see page 48).

Plying on a Wheel

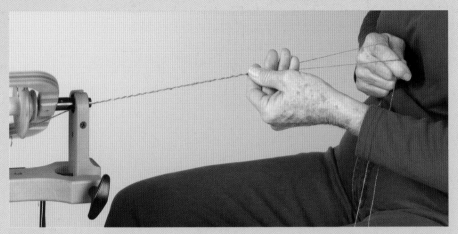

1. Slide your front hand back, keeping equal tension on both strands.

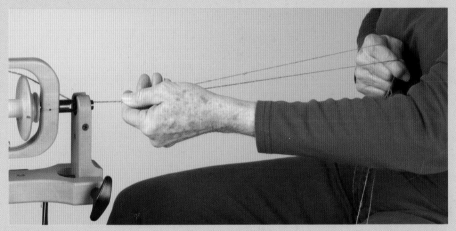

2. Allow the wheel to pull on the plied yarn, bringing your front hand forward and a new length of singles between your hands.

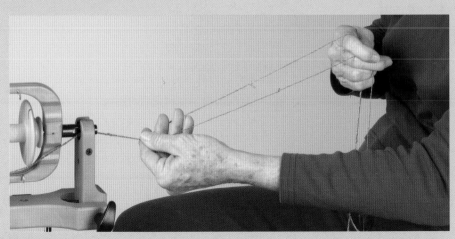

3. Straighten out any kinks like these by keeping the singles yarn under tension.

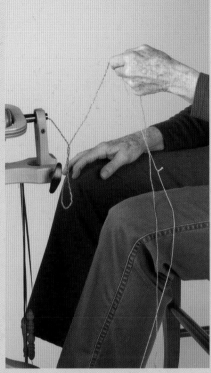

4. Relax the plied yarn to see how it compares with your sample.

Multiple Plies: Hold all three plies in your front hand so they twist together at the same point.

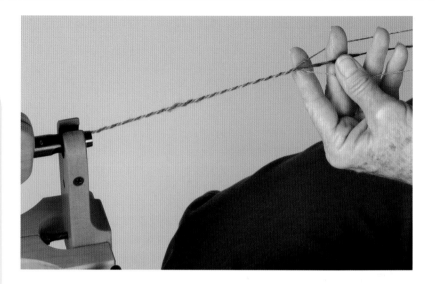

FIND THE PLYING RHYTHM

To make a beautifully plied yarn, you have to be consistent when you are plying. I figure out how many treadles it takes to reproduce my sample of balanced yarn by counting each time my right foot depresses the treadle as I bring the twist down the length of yarn between my hands. After I know how many treadles it takes, I count treadles for several minutes to develop the rhythm. Once I have the rhythm I don't need to count anymore.

Although the plying rhythm can be quick and fun, you must stop frequently to move the yarn to a new flyer hook. Plying fills up a bobbin quickly. Your bobbin will tell you when it is full; it will get harder and harder to wind the yarn onto the wheel. You may have to tighten the tension a little as the bobbin fills.

BREAK A YARN?

If one of your singles breaks while you are plying, you can stop and overlap the broken threads and start plying again. I prefer to tie the two ends together with an overhand knot and then start plying again. When I'm using the yarn, it's easy to find the knot and cut out that part, leaving only the smoother and stronger yarn. This is most important for weaving, when you need a strong yarn for a warp.

THE MORE THE MERRIER: MULTI-PLIED YARN

A 3-ply yarn makes a lovely round knitting yarn and really shows off pattern stitches, and it isn't much harder to spin than a 2-ply. You'll need to make a sample of your freshly spun singles folded into thirds. As you are spinning your singles, pull out a length of yarn, fold it in half, and then add one more strand of yarn. Break the yarn off and allow the twist to wrap the three strands together. This is your sample. Start with three bobbins on your kate and tie the yarns to your leader with an overhand knot. Just as with spinning a 2-ply, your back hand keeps all three singles under separate tension so the front hand can bring the twist into them. The front hand also has each yarn under separate tension and makes sure that all three twist together at the same point—you don't want a 2-ply with an extra wrap around it.

Use the same principle to make a 4-ply yarn, or even more . . . but keep in mind that you may run out of fingers to control the twist.

ALL PLIED UP

When your bobbin is full, it is time to wind the yarn into a skein. Let the wheel pull all of the plied yarn out of your hands and onto the bobbin. Leave the bobbin on your wheel but release the tension so the bobbin can turn freely. Stand several feet away to the side of the wheel, facing the bobbin, and wind off the yarn using a niddy-noddy (see page 66). The yarn does not go through the orifice. Secure the skein with several ties and admire your beautiful skein of plied yarn.

You may have heard that a balanced skein of yarn should hang open, but don't panic if your skein doesn't hang in a big open loop. It may twist back on itself, but that doesn't necessarily mean you have overtwisted it. If you have let your singles "rest" overnight (or over weeks, months, etc.) and then plied your yarn, the plying twist will be much more active than the spinning twist, and your plied skein may twist back on itself. It is true that a balanced skein of yarn should hang open, but that is after the twist has been set (see page 68), not just off the wheel. Don't worry until you have set the twist, because the warm water equalizes the twists. If you have matched the look of your sample, you should have a balanced yarn.

> You may have heard that a balanced skein of yarn should hang open, but don't panic if your skein doesn't hang in a big open loop.

CHAPTER EIGHT

Finishing Yarn

So after all that drafting, spinning, winding, and plying, your yarn must be finished, right? Well . . . not quite. You could start using your yarn right off the bobbin or spindle, but it isn't quite done yet. Setting the twist in your yarn is like having Cinderella's fairy godmother visit.

Niddy-noddies come in varying sizes, usually 1 to 2 yards (.9 to 1.8 m).

WHAT'S A NIDDY-NODDY?

A niddy-noddy looks like a confused capital letter I whose arms are at right angles to each other. Niddy-noddies come in different sizes; my favorite size has an 18-inch (46 cm) center and makes a 2-yard (1.8 m) skein. I can count the number of strands on one side of the skein, multiply by two, and know how many yards I have in my skein. Of course, I have several other niddies too, for making small samples and just because they are so darn cute.

Most niddy-noddies come apart into three pieces. If the arms of your niddy-noddy become too loose and want to fall off, try wrapping a little unspun wool around the ends to tighten up the joins. Don't glue the arms in this position; you may want to take your niddy apart when you go to a spinning group or for storage.

WIND SKEINS ON A NIDDY-NODDY

Hold your yarn and the center support of the niddy together in one hand. With the other hand wrap the yarn up over the top arm, down under the bottom arm, back up over the opposite top arm, and down under the last bottom arm. You will find yourself moving the niddy with a twist of your wrist to bring the next arm into position. In effect, you are making the niddy nod! You are just making a big circle of yarn with a half circle on each side of the niddy. Once you have established the pattern of winding, it becomes easier—just make sure you continue in the same path and don't crisscross the yarn. If it helps, you can number the ends of the arms one through four.

If you're lucky, after winding all of the yarn off your bobbin or spindle, the ends of yarn will meet and overlap slightly. If they do, tie them in a bow. If (as is more likely) your ends don't meet each other, bridge the gap with a piece of scrap yarn and tie them together. Don't take your skein off the niddy yet.

Cut several small lengths of scrap yarn and make some ties around your skein to keep it in order. If your skein isn't too big, two ties will be enough; just tie one loosely around the strands on one side of the niddy and tie the other on the opposite side. If your yarn is fine or if you have a large skein, make four ties—one on each side—and cross the scrap yarn through the skein to make ties in the shape of figure eights. Tie the ends of the scrap yarns with an overhand

Using A Niddy-Noddy

1. Wrap the yarn around each arm of the niddy-noddy in turn.

2. Keep wrapping the yarn in the same direction, without crisscrossing the strands.

3. The ends of your yarn will most likely not meet up perfectly.

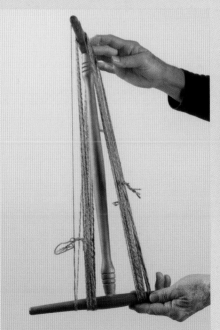

4. Tie a length of scrap yarn to bridge the gap between the ends.

5. Place one tie on each length of yarn on the niddy-noddy.

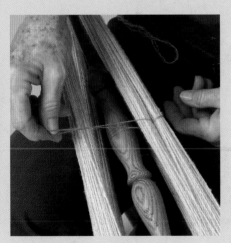

6. Pass the tie through the strands of yarn in a figure eight, then knot to secure.

Set Twist

Snap the skein between your hands to even out the twist and straighten the strands.

knot to make sure they won't come apart. I make my ties loose; if the tie is too tight, it might act as a resist if I dye the yarn, or I might inadvertently cut my yarn when taking off the tie. Now you can take the yarn off your niddy-noddy.

SETTING TWIST

Your yarn may be lovely, but after washing it will be exquisite. Water is the magic wand that relaxes the fibers, evens out the twist, and allows the fibers to bloom and regain elasticity. Wind your yarn into a skein and set the twist to admire the full beauty of the yarn you've made. All yarns look better after the twist is set. The easiest way to set twist is to simply wash the skeins. Fill a sink or bucket with warm to hot water and add a little dish detergent. Immerse your skein, then walk away and let the water and detergent do their job. Let the skein soak for 15 to 20 minutes before removing it from the water. Press the soapy water out of the skein gently but don't twist or agitate it. Drain the soapy water and fill the sink again with warm to hot water, this time adding a little distilled white vinegar (about a glug). Put the yarn in to soak for another few minutes, then remove the yarn and refill the sink again with clear water. Soak the yarn one last time to remove the salad smell.

Gently squeeze out the excess water by wrapping the skein in an old towel. Remove the skein from the towel and hold it between your hands. Give it a couple of sharp snaps to straighten out the strands and help even out the twist within the skein. What happens next depends on whether you have a singles yarn or a plied yarn.

Singles

At this point, your singles yarn will probably be all kinky and curly. Don't fret—most singles need a little weight to make them behave. Hang your skein up to dry and put a weight on it to straighten out the yarn. My favorite tool for weighting skeins is a plastic spray bottle filled partway with water; the spray lever hangs nicely on my skein, and I can add just enough water to weight the bottle and straighten out the kinks. Don't put too much weight on the skein; you want to leave some elasticity in the yarn.

Plied Yarn

After you have snapped your skein of plied yarn, it should hang naturally in a nice open loop. Just hang it over a hook and let it dry without weight. This is the time to look at your skein and decide whether it is balanced or not, because the spinning twist and plying twist were equalized in the wash. If the skein still twists after washing, you have added more twist in one direction than the other. You can tell by which way the skein twists (see page 15): If the yarn twists in a Z, you have more plying twist than spinning twist. If it twists in an S, you have more singles twist. Next time, try to make the amount of twists more even by matching your sample. Don't despair of this skein, though; a balanced yarn is easier to work with and has a smoother surface when knitted, but unbalanced yarns can be used with great effect, too.

In the right hands, overtwist can be an amazing tool, as in the work of spinner and artist Kathryn Alexander and her use of "energized yarns." In weaving, overspun yarns create incredible collapse fabrics.

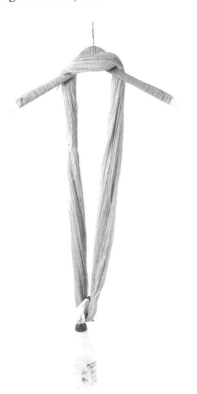

Weighting Singles: Hang a weight on singles as they dry to remove any kinks in the yarn.

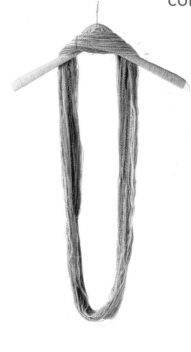

Balanced Yarn: This yarn hangs in an open loop, neither overspun nor overplied.

CHAPTER NINE

Know Your Spun Yarn

When you first begin spinning, turning a rolag into yarn without breaking feels like a huge accomplishment. As you practice, however, you develop higher expectations—you dream of spinning the exact yarn you want. You can make amazing yarn if you just relax and let the fibers flow.

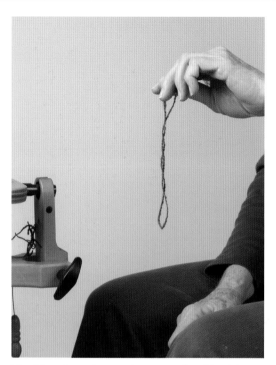

The "Rita Bracelet," a short sample of freshly spun yarn plied back on itself, is a wonderful tool.

A sample card with singles, plied yarn, and wheel settings can help you make consistent yarn.

SPINNING A CONSISTENT YARN

Although it's easy to sit down to spin and become lost in the mesmerizing action of turning fluff into yarn, you will very rarely spin all the yarn for a project in a single sitting. To spin a consistent yarn, you need to know that yarn. How thick is it? How much twist are you adding as you spin? If you know the answers to these questions you have a better chance of reproducing that yarn. The quickest and easiest way to compare today's yarn with last week's yarn is to have made a sample at the beginning of your project.

When you have created the yarn you want to spin for a project, spin a little of it (a yard or so), take that freshly spun yarn off your wheel or spindle, and let it twist back on itself. To keep this yarn handy, you can tie the ends together and make a loop or bracelet to attach to your wheel or wrist as a constant reminder. Rita Buchanan adds a bead to the loop to help recognize it as a sample.

As you spin, you can compare your new yarn to your "Rita Bracelet" (my name for it, not hers). Take a section of your new yarn, let it twist back on itself, and hold it next to the bracelet. Are the yarns the same size? Does the twist look the same? This is a quick and easy way to stay on course.

If you want more information, you don't need a magnifying glass or a microscope, but a ruler helps a lot.

WRAPS PER INCH

"Wraps per inch" is a very common way of describing handspun yarn. It tells you how fine or bulky the finished yarn is and it can be a helpful tool in selecting a pattern for your finished yarn. To measure wraps per inch (or w.p.i.), take your singles yarn and wrap it firmly but gently around a ruler or sett gauge for 1 inch (2.5 cm). (A sett gauge is a small tool, often shaped like a rectangle with a notch cut out but sometimes barrel-shaped, with a space 1 or 2 inches [2.5 or 5 cm] long designed for wrapping your yarn.) Make sure the strands nestle right next to each other, but don't overlap them. You shouldn't be able to see the ruler underneath the wraps. Then count the strands, and you have the wraps per inch.

Once you know how many w.p.i. you have in the sample, you can stop and check your yarn to see whether it is the same size. Don't worry if the two yarns aren't exactly the same; a little variation of up to 10 percent is fine, but you should be in the ballpark.

If you have fewer w.p.i. than in your sample, your yarn is too thick. To correct that, you can try one of the following:

§ Loosen the tension on your wheel, giving you more time to draft the fibers out farther.

§ On your wheel or spindle, draft out the fibers a little more so there are fewer of them in the drafting triangle.

If you have more w.p.i than in your sample, you yarn is too thin. Try one of these tricks to fatten it up:

§ Tighten the tension on your wheel.

§ On your wheel or spindle, open your twisting hand a little to let the twist grab more fibers in the drafting triangle.

Stopping and wrapping for 1 inch (2.5 cm) is a really accurate way to measure yarn, but it gets to be a bother. After you have the yarn the size you want, wrap the yarn several times around a piece of strong cardboard. As you spin you can stop and place your freshly spun yarn alongside your sample yarn and compare. It is a much faster way to check the thickness of your yarn. Do it often and your spinning will become more uniform.

TWIST PER INCH

There are different ways of measuring twist. One requires untwisting the yarn; another uses a protractor to measure the twist angle. Both are accurate but take time away from spinning. An easier way is to take a sample of freshly spun yarn (no more than 10 or 15 minutes old) and let it twist back on itself. See how the yarns twisting around each other produce bumps in the yarn? Hold that sample of yarn next to a ruler and count how many bumps there are in 1 inch (2.5 cm) and make a note of it. As you spin yarn for your project, stop occasionally to pull out a sample, let it twist back on itself, and see whether you are getting the same amount of twist by counting the

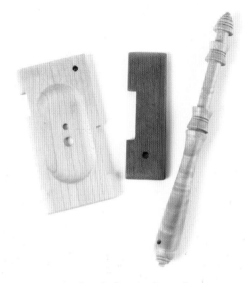

A sett gauge is handy for counting the wraps per inch.

Wrap the yarn closely around the ruler or sett gauge.

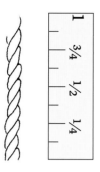

This length of yarn has 10 bumps per inch.

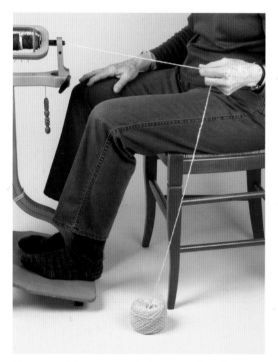

You can add or remove twist even after the yarn has been spun or plied.

bumps per inch. I keep my plied sample close by and just compare my new yarn to my sample to make sure I am consistent.

Bumps per inch may not be exactly the same as twists per inch, but it is an easy measurement and so is very useful. I punch a hole in the corner of my w.p.i. card and attach my bumps-per-inch bracelet. I write a little extra information on the card such as the type of fiber I'm using and the drive-wheel ratio of my wheel. Now this little card holds all the information I need to reproduce a yarn—it has wraps per inch, bumps per inch, and a sample of my balanced ply.

YARDS PER POUND

Yarn is also measured in yards per pound (y.p.p.). The higher the number of yards per pound, the thinner the yarn. A yarn that is 3,000 y.p.p. would be considerably thinner than one that measures 600 y.p.p.

To measure y.p.p., wind some yarn into a skein, measure the circumference of the skein (converting from inches or meters to yards if necessary), and count the number of strands in the skein. Multiply the number of strands by the circumference to find how many yards of yarn you have. Weigh the measured skein in ounces and multiply by 16 (the number of ounces in one pound). Divide the number of yards in the measured skein by the weight in pounds to find the y.p.p. (For example, imagine that you have wrapped your yarn into a 72-inch skein with 100 strands. The yarn is 7,200 inches, or 200 yards. If you have spun 4 ounces of fiber, or .25 pounds, then your yarn is 800 yards per pound.)

FIXING YARN WITH TOO MUCH TWIST (OR TOO LITTLE)

If you have spun a bobbin or spindle full of yarn with so much twist and so many kinks that it looks like you were spinning pigtails, you have overtwisted your yarn. Don't despair—you can fix it easily. Place the overtwisted bobbin on your lazy kate and put an empty bobbin on your wheel. Tighten the tension on your brake band so the yarn can be pulled on quickly, tie the twisted yarn to the leader of the working bobbin, and treadle counterclockwise (or the opposite direction from the way the yarn was spun).

Just letting the yarn flow through your hands usually removes enough twist, but if not, you can hold onto the yarn a little longer to help straighten out the really curly bits. Remember to change hooks frequently to fill the bobbin evenly.

The reverse is true too—if your yarn is too loosely plied, you can add more twist. This time you send the yarn back through the wheel in the same direction in which it was plied (counterclockwise).

Spindle spinners can do the same thing with their spindles. To fix yarn with too much twist, re-spin in the opposite direction; for too little twist, re-spin in the same direction from which the yarn was last spun. Use the same technique to add or take away plying twist. This works best before the twist is set, but you can do it afterwards as well.

CHAPTER TEN

Drafting In Depth

How fibers are prepared, and how twist enters those fibers, affects how your yarn looks and behaves. The two extremes are woolen and worsted, with lots of hybrids in between. These might seem like silly distinctions—woolen yarn is made of wool, and worsted is a medium-gauge yarn, right? In spinning, "woolen" and "worsted" have different meanings.

Woolen-spun yarn has a fuzzier finish in the skein and worked up.

Worsted-spun yarn is smoother and crisper than woolen-spun yarn.

WOOLEN-SPUN YARN

Woolen yarns are traditionally spun from shorter fibers (less than 4 inches [10 cm] long). All the fibers—long and short—are carded; the most woolen of woolen yarns is spun from rolags and spun with a long draw. Yarns made this way are fuzzy, lightweight, warm, and elastic. Woolen yarns are spun with twist between the hands, which allows the twist to grab the slightly disorganized fibers from the rolag. This creates little air pockets and allows some fiber ends to stick out.

When you knit or weave with woolen yarns, you will produce a soft, fuzzy fabric with bounce. Think of a Fair Isle sweater with patterns that seem to be painted with a watercolor brush; instead of being bold and crisp they are soft and blend into one another. A sweater, hat, or blanket would be a delightful choice for woolen-spun yarns. Woolen yarns also felt faster than worsted yarns do.

WORSTED-SPUN YARN

Worsted yarns are made from fibers that are combed and all the shorter fibers are removed. Combing also straightens all the remaining long fibers and lines them up to stand parallel to one another, like a platoon of soldiers standing at attention. Industry can comb many fibers, even short fibers like cotton, but hand-combed fibers are usually at least 3 inches (7.5 cm) long (and usually longer). Worsted yarns are spun with no twist between your hands. The fiber is drafted out, then the twist is smoothed into the fibers, locking them into place. A worsted yarn is smooth and strong and has more luster than a woolen yarn from the same fiber. Because of the way the twist grabs the fibers, it creates a denser, heavier yarn. I like to say that a pound of worsted yarn weighs more than a pound of woolen yarn, but what I really mean is that there should be more yards per pound of woolen yarn than worsted yarn if the yarns are the same size and fiber.

Since worsted yarn is so smooth and strong, it makes great socks and smooth handwoven fabric. A Norwegian ski sweater with its bold, graphic design would be superb in worsted yarn, as would an Aran sweater or any knitted article that requires crisp stitch definition.

WOOLEN AND WORSTED FIBER PREPARATIONS

The most woolen of woolen yarns is spun with a long draw from hand carded rolags. True worsted is spun from combed fibers with absolutely no twist between the hands. Then there are all the in-between yarns made through combinations of fiber preparation and drafting techniques. You can spin carded fiber with a worsted draw and get a smoother, denser yarn than you would if you spun it in a woolen manner. You can spin a combed top with twist between your hands, if you can draft at the same rate at which the twist is moving into the fibers, to produce a loftier smooth yarn. Add other types of fiber preparation like drum carding and flicking and spinning techniques like over the fold and the combinations multiply. There aren't any bad combinations as long as the yarn you spin is the yarn you want.

WOOLEN DRAFTING METHODS

In woolen-spun yarn, the twist runs into the fiber as it is being drafted, so there is twist between your hands. A true woolen yarn is spun from rolags with a long draw; carded roving works, too, but the yarn will not be quite as elastic.

Short Backward Draw

You already know how to do this technique—it is the first method described, in Chapters 3 and 6. After making a join and allowing a little twist between your hands, you pinch the yarn with the twist hand to prevent more twist from entering the drafting triangle and draft back a short distance with the fiber hand. The twist hand opens and allows more twist into the newly made yarn to stabilize it. The fiber hand then moves forward to allow the yarn to wind onto the bobbin. Then the process is repeated: pinch to control the twist, draft backward, release the pinch, and let the yarn wind on.

If you are using a spindle, the fiber hand moves away from the twisting hand. The twisting hand adds twist, then stays stationary while the fiber hands moves away from it. I find it easier to draft to the side instead of up.

The difference between woolen (top) and worsted yarn (bottom) is easy to see side by side.

Long-Draw Drafting

1. Pinch with the twist hand and draft with the fiber hand.

2. Keep moving the fiber hand back as you pinch and release with the twist hand.

3. You can comfortably do a long draw until your hand reaches your hip before letting the yarn wind on.

Short Forward Draw

You may be familiar with this method if you tried it on page 44: The twist hand pinches and then pulls forward just about a staple length of fiber. The fiber hand holds the fibers with a little tension while the twist hand is pulling forward, then relaxes a little as the twist hand moves back to just before the point of the drafting triangle. To spin an even yarn, be sure to pinch where the yarn is already formed, not in the drafting triangle (unless you want slubs in your yarn; in that case, go ahead and pinch in the triangle).

Use a short forward draw to get yarn onto the bobbin quickly without a lot of twist. The difference between this method and a worsted technique is that there is twist between the spinner's hands as the fiber is drafted.

When using a spindle, the fiber hand is above the spindle and the twist hand. After adding twist to the spindle the twist hand pulls fiber down to meet the twist, but there is twist between the hands.

Long Draw

In a long draw, the twist hand stays almost stationary while the fiber hand drafts backward at the same speed at which the twist moves up the yarn. The fiber hand stays just ahead of the twist and moves back at a constant rate. If the fiber hand goes too fast, the yarn will get thinner and thinner until it drifts apart and disappears into your bobbin. If the fiber hand goes too slowly, the twist will run amok, grab too many fibers, and keep you from drafting easily.

After you've made a join, allow a little twist into your fibers before pinching with the twist hand and drafting with the fiber hand. The twist hand stays stationary at a comfortable distance from the orifice, but it is quite active, pinching and then relaxing to control how fast the twist runs up the fiber. Meanwhile, the fiber hand is moving all the time, first backward to draft out the fibers, then forward to allow the yarn to wind onto the bobbin. The fiber hand has tension on the fibers as it moves back, but it opens a little as it releases the yarn onto the wheel. If the twist grabs in too many fibers and it is hard to draft, you can make the twist take a step backward by slightly unrolling the yarn counterclockwise with your twist hand. As you unroll with your twist hand, you should be able to draft backward with your fiber hand.

When you do the long draw, you can show off a little and draft back behind your body—it looks impressive—but your body won't like it for very long. Instead, try drafting back a comfortable distance (maybe to your hip bone), stop, make sure there is sufficient twist, and then let the yarn wind on.

This woolen draft is a great way to spin a soft, fluffy yarn quickly.

WORSTED DRAFTING METHODS

The most important thing to remember with worsted spinning is that there is *no twist between your hands.* For a true worsted yarn, start with combed fibers, either combed top or those you have prepared yourself (see page 110). If you are using your own combed fibers, they will probably draft quite easily, but combed top is another story. Top is quite dense and compact to begin with, and then it is made into large bumps and compacted even more. There are two schools of thought on how to treat combed top.

Pre-drafting Combed Top

Pull off a length of top a foot or two long, then divide it lengthwise into two or more long strips. Take one of the strips and pre-draft it, starting at one end of the strip and working to the other end and drafting one section at a time. I find it easier to pre-draft a strip a few times instead of trying to get to the size I want on the first pass. I draft out the whole piece and then do it again, each time making a thinner preparation. The size of yarn I want to spin dictates how much I draft out the fibers. When I'm done, I wrap the fibers into a little bird's nest, and then I'm ready to spin.

Join your fiber to the leader. After making the join, the twist hand pinches down to keep the twist out of the fiber between your hands. The twist hand pulls or drafts a section of fiber forward toward the wheel, and then—still keeping the twist in front of the twist hand—brings the twist back over the drafted-out fibers. Think, "Draft forward, smooth back." Each time the twist hand moves forward, it feeds a section of yarn onto the bobbin.

Watch the fibers between your hands. They shouldn't twist; if they do, then you know some twist has snuck behind your front

Pre-drafting Combed Top

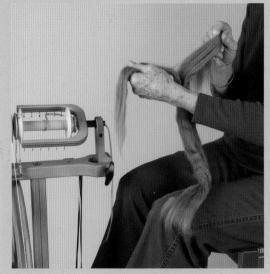

1. Split a piece of top lengthwise.

2. Draft the top several times until it is even and thin.

3. The twist hand pinches to keep twist in front of both hands.

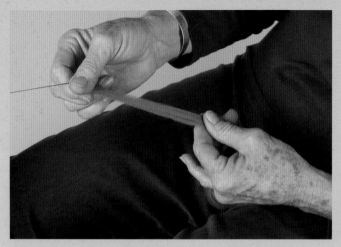 

1. Draft out the fibers between your twist hand and your fiber hand.

2. Smooth the twist back into the drafted fibers.

The most important thing to remember with worsted spinning is that there is *no twist between your hands.*

hand. You don't need to use the Vulcan Death Grip to keep the twist out, but you do need to keep it on the orifice side of your twist hand. If the twist gets between your hands, it will become harder and harder to draft as that wicked twist grabs all the parallel fibers and won't let go. Stop treadling and draft out some fibers until you get control of the twist. If that doesn't work, you may have to break the yarn and start over.

The fiber hand is working, too. During the drafting forward movement it is clamping down to control how many fibers leave and giving the twist hand something to draft against, then during the smooth back motion it relaxes a little so more fibers can move up to be drafted.

It's easy to get too much twist in worsted yarn because you can draft out less than a staple length each time you draft. If corkscrews start to occur, tighten your brake band a little to get the yarn onto the bobbin faster. If that doesn't work, you could go to a larger whorl.

If you are spinning combed top and the fibers just won't cooperate, break off your fiber and start spinning from the other end. It is often easier to spin in one direction than the other. When fibers are combed, care is taken so the fibers all lay in the same direction—cut

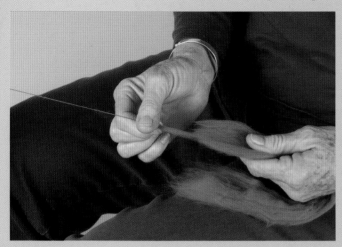

1. Join your leader to the top without pre-drafting.

2. Move your twist hand back and forth so that the fiber is drafted across the top.

end or tip end together—and sometimes one end drafts more easily than the other.

Try to coordinate your treadling to your drafting. As you treadle, draft the fiber forward with your twist hand. On the next treadle, smooth the twist back. This won't work for all sizes of yarns, but it is a lovely way to develop a rhythm.

Worsted Spinning with Undrafted Fibers

Do not strip or pre-draft the fiber. Join a length of top and spin with no twist between your hands, as described above, but slowly move your twist hand from one side of the fiber to the other. The fiber hand stays still and the twist hand gathers fiber, moving across the surface of the top. You have to make sure that no twist gets between your hands for this technique to work well. Spindle spinners can use the same technique as a short forward draw (see page 44), but don't allow any twist between your hands.

Over the Fold

If you are having trouble spinning combed fibers with a worsted draft, try spinning over the fold. To spin over the fold, you need

You don't need to use the Vulcan Death Grip to keep the twist out, but you do need to keep it on the orifice side of your twist hand.

1. Pull off one lock or staple length.

2. Drape the fiber over your index finger and hold both ends in your hand.

3. Let the twist run up and grab some fibers to join.

4. Pull the fibers forward with your twist hand.

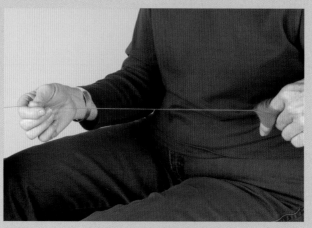

5. With practice, you can spin with a long draw over the fold.

combed fibers that are long enough to hang over your index finger with the ends clasped between your thumb and middle finger. Use a single combed lock of wool or, if you are using top, pull off just one staple length of undrafted fiber. Fold the staple length over the index finger of your fiber hand and hold it securely.

Fluff out your leader and hold it next to the folded fiber with the thumb of the fiber hand. Begin to treadle, letting the twist run up into the fiber and grab some fibers. After you've made a strong join, start doing a worsted draft with no twist between your hands (see page 81). As you spin, you may have to turn your fiber finger to keep the fibers flowing off the top and tip of your finger and from the center of the folded fiber. Pull the fibers forward toward the wheel with your twist hand, then smooth back as the twist runs up the fibers. The twist can't get out of control as easily with this drafting method because you have the front end of the fiber on one side of your finger and the tail end of the fiber on the other side. This technique works for spindle spinning, too; just keep the twist on the spindle side of your twist hand.

This yarn won't be quite as strong and smooth as true worsted, but it is a lot easier to spin and produces lovely, smooth yarn. The downside is that you will have to make a lot of joins because you can only use only one staple length of fiber at a time. (Look at it as an opportunity to practice your join technique.)

Once you are comfortable spinning over the fold with a worsted draw, try a short forward draw with twist between your hands. The fibers won't draft out quite as smoothly as a true worsted yarn, but you will still produce a smooth loftier yarn. This is one of those in-between yarns: it has combed fibers, but a woolen draft.

You can even do a long draw from over-the-fold fibers. After you've made a join, start drafting backward with your fiber hand and control the twist with your twist hand.

Spinning top or locks over the fold produces a yarn with woolen and worsted characteristics.

CHAPTER ELEVEN

Using Your Handspun Yarn

I really can't say enough about the pleasure of using your handspun. First you have the enjoyment of creating the yarn and then the satisfaction of turning it into fabric. Using your yarn to create a garment or other article of useful beauty completes the spinning process. Just as a chef needs to taste a dish to see whether the ingredients are in balance, using your yarn will make you a better spinner.

As the yarn slips through your fingers, you'll feel the twist and how it affects the fabric you are creating. Your eyes will see the drape of the fabric and the way the color reflects the light. As you wear your handspun, you can see whether the garment holds its shape and how it feels on your body. All of this information will be available the next time you sit down at the wheel or pick up a spindle.

I didn't know this when I first learned to spin, so for a while just making yarn was enough. Lots of yarn, skeins and skeins and skeins. (In fact, I learned to make baskets just to have a place to put the yarn.) When the baskets got full, I started making things out of those skeins, but the projects I made didn't please me as much as my yarn did. Often I couldn't find the right project for my yarn, or there wasn't enough yarn, or the color wasn't right . . . I needed a new approach, so I reversed the process—I chose a project and then spun the yarn for it. What a difference! Instead of being underwhelmed, I was overjoyed! I loved my finished piece. I became a convert and a true believer in spinning for a purpose.

Generous knitted swatches can tell you so much about working with your homespun.

This shawl records Ruth Hollowell's progress as a spinner. At the end of Spinning 1, Ruth decided to knit lace, so she prepared a fleece and began spinning a two-ply yarn. She designed the shawl as she knitted from the center out, and by the time she reached the edges her spinning had improved markedly. The airy yarn shows the lace patterns beautifully, and the center-out pattern hides any gauge changes.

Roxana Bartlett's colorful vest is handdyed, handspun, and handknitted. It was knitted from side to side in a slip-stitch pattern to show the beautiful range of colors.

Keep your sample card and swatch together as a record of your project.

Spinning for a purpose involves planning; first you choose a project, and then you decide what kind of yarn you want to spin. Make a list of the qualities you want your yarn to have. Then decide how you can spin the yarn to meet your criteria:

§ How should it be prepared?

§ What fiber?

§ What size?

§ How many plies?

§ How much?

So many good questions. Make some choices and spin a little yarn to match your decisions. Then make a swatch! I know you think you don't have enough time, money, fiber, or desire to sample, but do it anyway. You won't be sorry. Knit a swatch or weave a sample. Do you love it? Great, then spin some more and you are on your way. If you don't care for your sample, figure out why:

§ Is the fabric too stiff or so soft it won't hold its shape?

§ Does the yarn not work with the pattern? How can you make it better?

§ Should you prepare the fiber a different way?

§ Does it need more or less twist?

§ Should you change the number of plies?

I know this process sounds like a lot of work, but trust me, deciding that a sample doesn't work is much easier than realizing you will never wear the vest you just finished.

For quick success, try a small project for your first handspun, such as a hat, scarf, or mittens. They only take a few ounces of fiber and not too many hours of spinning. But before you spin all the yarn for the project, make a sample to be sure your finished yarn matches your project. Spin some yarn you think will work for your project. Measure the wraps per inch and the twist per inch (see page 72), and make a sample card. Pull off a length of yarn, let it ply back on itself, and keep it with the sample card so you will also have a sample of a balanced plied yarn. Spin and ply a little more yarn the same size, then wash it and set the twist (see page 68).

Washing your yarn before making your project is crucial. Yarn that you thought was as fine as froghair when you spun it may turn into worsted weight after a bath. Some fibers really loft or pouf up once they are washed.

Use this yarn to knit a swatch, a healthy one at least 6 inches (15 cm) square. Measure the stitches in the center of the swatch to check your gauge but remember that just getting gauge is not enough. Do you like the fabric? How does it feel? How does it drape? Try different size needles or hooks and stitches and make a fabric you love.

USING HANDSPUN FOR WRITTEN PATTERNS

If you are using a pattern that calls for a commercial yarn and you can find that yarn for comparison, use it as a guide for making your own yarn. Spin and ply a small amount of yarn that size, set the twist, and make a swatch. If it doesn't come out right the first time, try again—think of it as a challenge. When you do get gauge, and you like the fabric, spin the amount of yarn the pattern calls for plus a little extra. Don't rely on the weight of the yarn called for in the pattern; yardage is always the most accurate gauge of how much yarn you will need, and you can measure that with your niddy-noddy. Always spin a little more yarn than you think you need. Call it yarn insurance!

If you can't find a sample of the yarn the pattern uses, see the yarn sizes chart on page 93 and use that as a guide for spinning your yarn. If a pattern calls for a worsted-weight yarn that knits up at 5 stitches per inch (2.5 cm), spin some yarn that measures about 12 wraps per inch when it is plied and the twist is set.

BREAK FREE! DESIGN YOUR OWN PATTERN

If you want to design your own garment, there are even more choices. Ann Budd's books *The Knitter's Handy Book of Patterns* and *The Knitter's Handy Book of Sweater Patterns* are a spinner's delight. She gives patterns in multiple gauges, so all you have to do is spin some yarn, knit a swatch to measure your gauge, and plug the results into

A hat, scarf, or pair of mittens is a good use of your first handspun.

This garter stitch scarf, knitted lengthwise, shows off several handspun yarns.

her designs. Elizabeth Zimmerman's percentage formula (from her book *Knitting Workshop*) is also a boon for spinners. For the truly adventurous designer who would rather make up her own pattern, there are cards available from several sources that will give you approximate yardages of how much yarn you need to knit a project depending on your gauge.

NOTES ON WEAVING

If you are spinning to weave, knowing the wraps per inch will help you choose a sett for your yarn. As a weaver you are used to wrapping your yarn to determine your sett. If your handspun warp yarn is a little inconsistent, wrap 2 inches (5 cm) instead of just 1 inch (2.5 cm) to determine your ends per inch (e.p.i.). Just remember to adjust your figures to get back to 1 inch. For example, if your yarn wraps 40 times over 2 inches, divide that in half to get the wraps per inch (20) and then divide in half again to get the e.p.i. (10).

If you are spinning for warp, make sure your joins are strong. A plied yarn will handle the abrasion that occurs when the threads go through the heddles and the reed better than a singles will. Use a larger dent reed than your ends per inch to protect your warp from being rubbed to death. For example, use two threads in a 6-dent reed instead of one thread in a 12-dent reed. (Weft yarn doesn't have to be as sturdy, so let your imagination run wild.)

One of the hardest things in the world to do is to sample before you weave a project. With knitting, you can just unravel the swatch and reuse the yarn. Not so with weaving. But it is far better to discover your warp sett isn't quite right or the weft is too heavy on a sample than after you have spun all the yarn.

SPIN ON!

Once your sample works, spin the yarn you need and knit, crochet, or weave away. Spinning is about possibilities, and the more you spin the more you learn, leading to even more possibilities. Not all of the yarns we spin will be grand successes, and some may even be duds, but we never know until we try. We have the ability to bring out the best qualities of the fiber we are spinning and then create a fabric that is so much more than the sum of its parts.

TIPS FOR WORKING WITH HANDSPUN

§ Don't stretch the yarn when measuring.

§ When measuring thicker yarn, you will get a more accurate
   result by wrapping 2 inches (5 cm) instead of 1 inch (2.5 cm). If
   your yarn varies in size, wrap 3 or 4 inches and take the average.

§ Needle sizes are only a suggestion; only a gauge swatch will tell
   you what size needle you need.

§ Remember, just getting the correct gauge is not enough. The
   way the fabric looks and feels is the most important thing.

APPROXIMATE YARN SIZES			
Yarn Size	Wraps per Inch (WPI)	Recommended Gauge (st/in)	Recommended Needle
Laceweight	18 or more	8 or more	U.S. 00–2 (2–2.75 mm)
Fingering-weight	16	6–8	U.S. 0–3 (2–3.25 mm)
Sportweight	14	6	U.S. 4–6 (3.5–4 mm)
Double-knitting	13	5½	U.S. 5–7 (3.75–4.5 mm)
Worsted-weight	12	4½–5	U.S. 7–8 (4.5–5 mm)
Aran-weight	11	4	U.S. 9–10 (5.5–6 mm)
Bulky-weight	10	3–3½	U.S. 10–11 (6–8 mm)

From Sheep to Spinning

The best (and ultimately easiest) way to get the yarn you want is to make it the way you like it from the very beginning. Only you know what kind of yarn you want to spin.

Preparing your own fiber may seem like a time-consuming process when you really just want to make great yarn. When you can buy so many lovely batts, rovings, and other preparations of fiber and begin spinning them immediately, why go through the bother of choosing, washing, and carding or combing the wool yourself?

The best (and ultimately easiest) way to get the yarn you want is to make it the way you like it from the very beginning. Only you know what kind of yarn you want to spin—thick and springy, soft and fuzzy, fine and sleek—and by choosing everything from the sheep to the method of preparation, you come closest to getting the exact end product you have in mind. There is also a special connection with wool you have prepared yourself—you may know the name and breed and age of the sheep that grew it, remember the scent of fresh lanolin, and be amazed by the transformation from freshly shorn fleece to clean, fluffy clouds of wool. Fleece you have prepared yourself will have a softer hand and more life than a similar fleece that has been commercially processed. Think of it as the difference between a meal prepared at home and dorm food.

BUYING A FLEECE

Before you buy a fleece, remember that not all fleeces are created equal. Some sheep are raised for their meat and not much attention is paid to the quality of the fleece, whereas a spinners' flock has been raised with the emphasis on the fleece. Sheep growers who breed sheep for their fleece have taken extra care so the fleece will be strong, beautiful, and clean. Many of these sheep wear coats to keep the dirt and weeds out of their fleece. Shearing is done carefully to avoid second cuts and to keep the fleece in the best shape.

A fleece from a spinners' flock will cost more but is well worth the extra money.

Types of Sheep

For the purposes of spinning, sheep are generally divided into categories depending on the length and fineness of the fiber. There are two ways wool is measured for fineness: micron count and the Bradford count. Micron count is the easiest to understand: it is how fine an individual wool fiber is, measured in microns; the smaller the number, the finer the fleece. The Bradford count was developed more than 200 years ago and refers to the number of 560-yard skeins that could be spun from a pound of wool. A Corriedale fleece with a count of 55s would theoretically yield 55 skeins of yarn, each 560 yards long. No one actually spins the fleece to test it, but experienced sheep growers can tell by looking at a fleece what the count would be.

Fine wool breeds include sheep like Merino and Rambouillet. Fibers from these sheep are very fine (17 to 23 microns) and short (2 to 4 inches [5 to 10 cm] long). The Bradford count falls in the 62/90s range. Fine wools need special preparation before spinning because they felt easily and have an abundance of lanolin. The crimp is very tight in these fleeces, so the yarn is extra elastic, soft, and puffy. Yarn from fine wools is good for baby clothes and garments worn next to the skin.

Medium wool comes from breeds such as Corriedale and Columbia. Fibers from this category are usually in the 23 to 31 micron range and are 3 to 6 inches (7.5 to 15 cm) long with a Bradford count of 50/60s. The crimp is still well defined, but not as compact. The yarn, while not as soft as a fine wool, is stronger. Yarns spun from these breeds make excellent sweaters, mittens, and hats.

Down breeds have lovely English names like Dorset, Suffolk, and Southdown. The word "down" refers to their place of origin, the Downs of England, not the softness of their fleece. These sheep are generally bred as meat sheep, although their wool can be quite nice. The fibers are short (2 to 4 inches [5 to 10 cm]) and the micron count varies from 23 to 40 microns. Depending on the breed, the Bradford count can range from 54/60s in a finer Southdown to 36/56s in the coarser Dorset. Crimp is present in down breeds, but not well organized in the lock. Yarn spun from down breeds has a matte surface,

Fine Merino locks

Medium Corriedale locks

is quite elastic, and doesn't felt easily. Wool from these sheep makes good sweaters, socks, and mittens.

The long wools or lustre breeds include sheep such as Lincoln, Romney, and Border Leicester. As the name implies, the wool from these sheep has a luster, like mohair. The fibers from these breeds are longer and coarser, and the crimp is now a soft, open wave. The micron count for these sheep is in the 29 to 40 range and the fibers can be 5 to 12 inches (12.5 to 30.5 cm) long. The Bradford count for these wools can range from 36/50s. Yarn from long wools is not as elastic as from the finer breeds, but it is much stronger. Tapestries, rugs, and sturdy outerwear are good choices for long-wool breeds.

Other breeds include ancient varieties such as Karakul, Navajo Churro, and Shetland. These sheep often have two coats, a long, coarse outer coat and a soft, short undercoat. With dual-coated fleece you can spin a smooth, strong, coarse yarn from the outer coat and a softer warm yarn from the undercoat.

As with puppies, not all sheep are purebreds, and some of the very best spinning fiber comes from crosses (mixtures of several different breeds). As you become more familiar with different fleeces, you will learn to distinguish the properties of each. Don't worry too much about the breed name; just look at the fleece yourself to see whether it will work for the project you have in mind.

For more information on sheep breeds, consult the excellent reference *In Sheep's Clothing* by Nola and Jane Fournier.

Choosing a First Fleece

Your first fleece should be a medium-wool breed like Corriedale with a staple length of 3 to 5 inches (7.5 to 12.5 cm). Looking at a lock or staple of wool will tell you many things about the fleece it comes from.

§   The lock should have an even crimp over its entire length; uneven crimp can be a sign of a break or weak spot.

§   Take the lock in both hands and tug on it quickly to test it for strength. It should not break, and it should spring back when you relax your hold on it.

Long Lincoln locks

Dual-coated Karakul locks

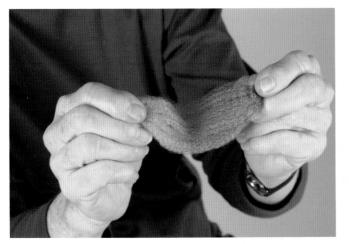 

Tug the ends of the lock to test for strength and listen for a soft ping.

§ Listen to the lock when you test it for strength—it should have a little musical sound to it, almost like crystal. If the lock isn't strong, it won't make a "ping" but will sound more like a dull thud.

§ It is a good idea to pull three or four small locks from different parts of a fleece and compare them for consistency in the crimp. If some areas of the fleece are very crimpy and some very straight, it will be difficult to spin a consistent yarn.

§ Ask the person you are buying the fleece from whether it has been coated. A coat on the sheep will keep the fleece clean and free of vegetable matter.

§ Ask whether the fleece has been skirted. Skirting removes all the really dirty, matted fibers like the belly wool, dung tags (just what they sound like), and sometimes neck wool, which is often matted and contaminated with feed.

Don't worry too much about the breed name; just look at the fleece yourself to see whether it will work for the project you have in mind.

PREPARING THE FLEECE

Once you've gotten your fleece home, take it out and admire it. (If you live with dogs and cats, they will be happy to help.) Spread out an old sheet, outside if possible, and open up your fleece. If there are sections of fleece that have been contaminated with a lot of weed

THINGS TO LOOK FOR WHEN CHOOSING A FLEECE

Cleanliness

Sheep are not especially clean animals, but if a fleece is stained, excessively dirty, or full of vegetable matter, you may want to avoid it. Vegetable matter such as hay and weeds must be removed by hand, and this can be very time-consuming.

Strength

Test a small lock of wool for strength. Tender wool will often break while carding or spinning. Sheep that have had some physical stress, such as illness or lambing, may have a weak spot in their wool.

Quality of Shearing

When the shearer doesn't cut close enough to the skin the first time, he has to make a second pass. This produces second cuts—short pieces of fleece—making lumpy bumps in your handspun.

Skirting

A well-skirted fleece will have all the dung tags and belly wool removed. When you are buying by the pound, why pay for poop?

Uniformity of Crimp and Texture

The crimp should be fairly uniform throughout the fleece and also in the individual lock.

Greasiness

The amount of lanolin in a fleece will vary greatly depending on the breed. If a fleece is stored for a long time before it is sold, the lanolin can congeal and be difficult to remove. A fresh fleece—a year or less off the sheep—is best.

Avoid a fleece that has. . .
"Cotty" Wool

Fleece that has started to mat while on the sheep is very hard to card and spin into an even yarn.

"Tippy" Fleece

The tips of some fleece may be overweathered and become dry and brittle. Sometimes the tips will break off or accept dye differently. Test for tippy fleece by gently tugging at the tips—if they are weak, they will break off.

Musty Smell

If the sheep was sheared when the weather was damp and the fleece was stored before it was totally dry, mildew will damage the fiber. Never accept a fleece with moths or mildew.

Kemp

These are short, brittle, hairy fibers in the fleece that don't blend into the yarn or dye well.

seeds or hay, pull them out and throw them away or felt them into cat toys. If there are areas of really dirty, matted wool, they go, too. Be careful, though, to leave the fleece in lock formation as much as possible. The locks protect the fibers from felting.

You can either spin your beautiful fleece just as it is ("in the grease") or wash it. Spinning in the grease keeps the lanolin in the yarn, but it also keeps all the dirt in. After you've spun the yarn, it is harder to get that lanolin out, and over time your yarn can become stiff and sticky. A washed, clean fleece drafts out smoothly, takes dye evenly, and is softer and easier to spin.

Fleece before washing

Washing Fleece

Some instructions for preparing fleece call it **scouring** the wool. That sounds so very harsh, as though you were scrubbing and pounding the fleece. Nothing is further from the truth—you want to treat the fleece gently, and the finer the fiber the more care it needs. To wash fleece, you need very hot water and a mild detergent (the one you use to handwash dishes will work nicely). Have a bottle of white vinegar on hand.

You will need a container to keep the fleece together; a laundry basket with holes on the sides and on the bottom works well, or use a few lingerie bags. (Just don't plan on ever using those bags for lingerie again.) Try to keep the locks together and well organized. You need the wool to be in locks for combing, and keeping the locks together also makes it easier to tease the wool before carding. If there is too much fleece to fit into one container, gently pull sections of the fleece apart to divide it.

A laundry basket can hold the fleece for washing.

1. Place the fleece in the basket or lingerie bag. Don't put it in the sink or tub yet.

2. Fill a tub or sink with very hot water—it should be too hot to keep your hand in it for very long. If your tap water isn't hot enough, heat up some extra water in a tea kettle and add it to the sink or tub.

3. Add the detergent to the hot water; use more than you would if you were doing dishes. The water should feel slippery because of the detergent.

Place the fleece in a lingerie bag dedicated to this purpose.

Keep the unwashed fleece organized in lock formation.

Leave the fleece to dry in a well-ventilated area.

4. Put your container of fleece in the water, push it down below the surface, and then leave it alone. Don't swoosh it around. You're already working with hot water and soap, two of the three elements needed to make felt; unless you want an unspinnable clump, avoid the third element, agitation.

5. Let the wool sit in the hot water for about 15 minutes, then lift the container out of the water and let the water drain out of the tub or sink. Don't leave the container in the tub while you are draining out the water—sometimes even that is too much agitation and the wool can begin to felt.

6. Refill the tub with hot water and do a second wash just like the first one, this time using less detergent.

7. To rinse the fleece, fill the tub a third time with hot water and this time pour in a good healthy glug of white distilled vinegar. Place the wool in the tub to soak for 5 to 10 minutes. Wool is a protein fiber and is damaged by alkali; vinegar neutralizes the alkalinity of soaps and detergents.

8. Rinse once more in hot water to remove the vinegar odor.

9. If you have washed just a little fleece, you can wrap it in old towels and squeeze out the excess moisture. If you have a lot of fleece, you may want to use your top-loading washing machine to spin out the excess water; a front-loading washer may not work for this step and may felt your fleece. Put the fleece (in a lingerie bag) in your washer and turn on the spin cycle. If your spin cycle adds cold water, turn off the cold water tap so it can't felt your fiber. Just remember to turn the cold water back on for your next wash. The lingerie bag protects both your fleece and your washing machine.

10. Spread your damp fiber out and let it dry. The more air that can circulate around the fiber the faster it will dry. A sweater dryer works well for this or use some old towels. It may take several days to dry, but when your fleece is clean and dry it will be a delight to spin. Although it looks tempting, wool is weaker when wet, so wait until it is dry to spin it.

WASHING FLEECE, THE ADVENTUROUS EDITION

At bottom, a spinner accidentally sent her fleece through the whole wash cycle; at top, an impatient spinner tried to help his fleece dry by tumbling it in the dryer. Disaster!

You may have heard or read that you can use your washing machine to wash your fleece. You can, with care, if your machine is a top-loader.

1. Use lingerie bags to contain the fleece; you don't want it to wind up in the washer's innards.

2. Fill up the tub with hot water and add mild detergent. *Turn off the machine.*

3. Put in the lingerie bags, close the lid to keep in the heat, and let the fleece soak for 10 to 15 minutes.

4. Take out the fleece, drain the washer, refill it, and follow the instructions for washing in the tub on page 99, always remembering to *turn off the machine.* If you forget and let the machine agitate, your beautiful fluffy wool will turn into a felted cat toy. The dryer will do similar nasty things to fleece, too.

Storing Fleece

Now that you have a huge pile of fluffy, clean fleece, where to put it? I store my fleece in clear plastic storage bins. The bins are stackable and clear, so I can keep them out of the way but easily see what's inside. Most importantly, the tight-fitting lid keeps the fleece safe from marauding kitties, puppies, and other beasties. You can also store the washed fleece in brown paper bags, cardboard boxes, or cloth bags if you have a dry, secure place. Don't store fleece in plastic bags because the bag can contract and expand as the temperature changes and felt the fleece. Don't store dirty fleece—moths are more attracted to dirty fleece, so washing fleece is the best way to make sure they don't take up residence. Before you put fleece away, make sure it is dry. Wool can hold up to 30 percent of its weight in water before it feels damp. A mildewed fleece is a cause for tears.

Don't store dirty fleece—moths are more attracted to dirty fleece, so washing fleece is the best way to make sure they don't take up residence.

3. Gently pull the locks apart, allowing any seeds, rough spots, or debris to fall onto the newspaper.

1. Place the unteased fleece on one side of you and a container for the teased fleece on the other side, with newspaper spread on the floor in front of you.

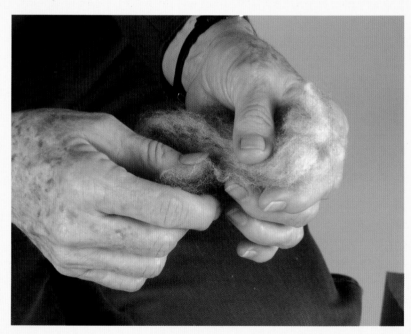

2. Plucking out this second cut now will prevent it from becoming an uneven bumpy spot in your yarn.

4. As you pull the locks apart, check the cut ends carefully for bits of fiber that tangle or mat. Remove them.

Teasing Fleece

Once the fleece is dry, it is time to prepare it for spinning. To make carded fiber, start by teasing the wool, or opening up the locks and removing any undesirable bits. A lot of people find teasing wool boring, and I will admit I would never do it if I didn't get to spin the wool I had teased. But teasing thoroughly before carding makes the finished yarn so much nicer.

To tease the wool, place a container of clean fleece on one side of where you plan to sit, newspaper on the floor in front of you, and an empty bag on the other side. Grab a few locks and gently pull them apart. As you open up the fibers, any debris in the fleece will fall onto the newspaper. If you see any weed seeds, matted areas, or second cuts, get rid of them. (Second cuts are little bits of fleece that result when the shearer doesn't get close enough to the skin on the first pass and goes back for a "second cut." You want to remove these short fibers because they will make **noils**—little lumps and bumps—in your yarn.) If your wool is still in lock formation, look at the lock and notice the cut end (the one closest to the sheep) and the tip end (the one on the outside). Noils are often formed at the cut end; if some of the fibers do not pull apart easily because of tangles and mats, toss them aside. You won't like the way they spin. It is okay to not spin every bit of your fleece—you can use it for felt, your compost heap would love to have a little fiber, or you can just throw it away.

When I am spinning a fine yarn for a lace scarf, I tease more thoroughly than when I am spinning yarn for a rug. As you tease open the fibers, you will produce a lovely fluffy mass. If you wanted to, you could spin this fluff, but for a more uniform yarn, carding is the next step.

Carding Fiber

Carding fiber is the most common method of preparing wool for woolen spinning. It aligns the fibers in more or less the same direction, but it doesn't remove shorter hairs. Spinners can use handcards or drumcarders to card clean fleece.

Handcards

Handcards look like oversized dog brushes. They come in pairs and are covered in fine wire teeth. Standard wool cards have about 72

> Once the fleece is dry, it is time to prepare it for spinning. To make carded fiber, start by teasing the wool, or opening up the locks and removing any undesirable bits.

Cotton, regular, and coarse handcards

1. Hang a bit of fleece on the handcard.

2. Move across the handcard, placing more fleece on the teeth.

3. Touch the bottom of the working carder to the bottom of the dressed carder.

4. Gently straighten out the fibers, brushing with a rocking motion.

5. Continue to pull the cards apart until there is no fiber connecting them.

6. What not to do: Beginning a new stroke without finishing the last one will fold the fibers over and make a tangled mess.

7. The dressed card with its "beard."

8. Brush just the "beard" of the dressed card, not even touching the card itself.

9. All the fibers have been transferred to the working card.

10. Hold the dressed card in your lap.

11. Roll the carded fibers toward you.

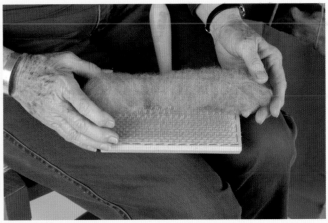

12. A finished rolag.

Although the teeth of the handcards may look uncomfortable, carding should not be a painful experience. You are just straightening out the fibers and transferring them to the other carder.

teeth per square inch (2.5 cm) and work well with most breeds of wool. Cards coarser than 72 teeth per square inch are not as versatile. Fine cards are also available for fine wools, alpaca, and kid mohair. These cards have more teeth per square inch (about 112) and the teeth are made of finer wire. Cotton cards have even finer teeth and are set closer together, as many as 208 per square inch. Cotton cards are wider and can also be used for fine fibers like cashmere. Cards come with either curved or straight backs; most people seem to prefer curved cards, but both kinds work equally well.

There are several different ways to card; I wasn't very good at the traditional method, so I came up with my own version. It is unorthodox, but it produces a fiber preparation that is easy to spin (to make rolags in the traditional manner, see Carol Rhoades's excellent article in the Fall 2001 issue of *Spin-Off* magazine.)

Pick up a card in your nondominant hand with the handle pointing up. In this position, the teeth on the card are pointed up and look like little hooks. Take a handful of teased fleece in your other hand and put it on the card just as if you were hanging a jacket on a hook. As you place the fiber on the card, pull down a little just to secure the fibers on the teeth. Starting at one side of the card, touch the fleece to the hooks and pull down; some of the fleece will remain on the card. Move over to the next empty spot on the card and hang another part of the fleece the same way, working your way across the card until it is full. You have just "charged" or "dressed" the card.

Although the teeth of the handcards may look uncomfortable, carding should not be a painful experience. You are just straightening out the fibers and transferring them to the other carder. Rest the dressed carder on one knee and with your dominant hand pick up the second (working) carder. Touch the bottom of the working carder to the bottom of the dressed carder and gently brush or card out the fibers using a rocking stroke (as though blow-drying someone's hair in an exaggerated flip). As you do this, some of the fibers will transfer to the working carder. Complete the stroke; don't stop while there is still fiber connecting the cards. Be gentle—think of combing a small child's tangled hair. The cards' teeth should not really mesh; it isn't necessary to scrape the fiber from one card to the other. On the second stroke, move the working carder up the dressed carder and straighten out and transfer those fibers, again making sure you complete the pass and don't fold the fibers over on themselves. After several strokes most of the fiber should be on the working carder.

Now the nontraditional part: Instead of transferring the fiber back to the first card, just change hands. The now-empty card becomes the working card, the full card becomes the dressed card, and the whole process starts all over again. Now the dressed card looks like it has a beard. Using a rocking motion, take the working card and start brushing the "beard," not even touching the dressed card at first. After those fibers have been transferred, the working carder works its way up the dressed carder again until all the fibers are transferred. Then change hands again. Usually three transfers are sufficient to straighten out the fibers. The fibers should be somewhat parallel now and quite straightened out.

It is time to make a **rolag**. Place the dressed card on your lap with the handle pointing toward your body. Starting at the bottom edge of the card, roll the fibers toward you as though making a little jelly roll of fiber. Make several rolags so you will have a nice supply when it is time to spin.

As you practice handcarding, try dressing the carder with different amounts of fiber to see what feels comfortable. You want to be as efficient as possible while still doing a thorough job. The size of finished yarn you want will help determine the size of your rolag; you can't make a fat yarn from a thin rolag, and a fat rolag will require more drafting to make a thin yarn. Carding takes time, and it is easy to be impatient when what you really want to do is spin. But carding carefully is well worth the time it takes—your spinning is only as good as your preparation.

Drumcarder

Using a drumcarder is much faster than handcarding, but not necessarily better. Working with small amounts of fiber and handcards produces lofty, easy-to-spin rolags, but if you have a large project in mind or limited time, a drumcarder can be your best friend (next to your spinning wheel, of course). A drumcarder is an expensive tool, but it can cut down hours of handcarding and can quickly blend colors and fibers into luscious batts. Do some research before you get a drumcarder to choose the size of carder and carding cloth that will best suit your needs. Some carders have finer teeth on the carding cloth,

The size of finished yarn you want will help determine the size of your rolag; you can't make a fat yarn from a thin rolag, and a fat rolag will require more drafting to make a thin yarn.

1. Place the fiber in the tray a little at a time.

2. The big drum is nearly full of fibers, while the licker-in is empty.

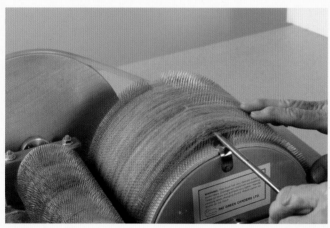

3. When the big drum is full, slide the doffer between the drum and the batt.

4. It may be necessary to lift off the batt in sections.

5. Separate the fibers to free the batt.

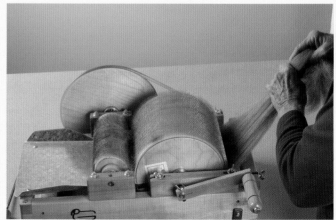

6. Peel the batt off the large drum.

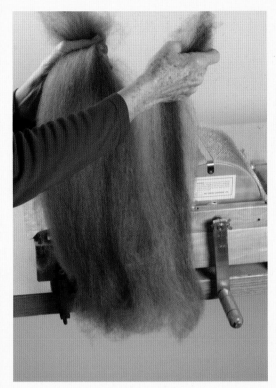

8. Pass each of the strips through the drumcarder again.

7. Divide the batt into long strips.

some coarser. Some carders have interchangeable drums for different fibers. Like all tools, drumcarders need to be used with care.

To get the best results from your drumcarder, follow the manufacturer's instructions on how to adjust the drums. Most carders have the drums adjusted so that the teeth do not touch and a piece of paper can fit between the two drums. (The Louet drumcarder is an exception—the drums are not adjustable and the teeth touch.)

Be sure to use clean wool on your carder; you don't want to gum up the carding cloth or get dirt in the mechanism. Tease your wool well, removing second cuts and debris. The better the preparation, the better the yarn.

Feed small amounts of fiber into the carder by putting them in the tray area closest to the small drum (licker-in). The licker-in will pick up the fibers from the tray and deposit most of them on the big drum. If a lot of fibers are staying on the licker-in, stop and make

A drumcarder is an expensive tool, but it can cut down hours of handcarding and can quickly blend colors and fibers into luscious batts.

Comb with a handcard: Hold a lock of wool firmly against a handcard and draw it through the card.

sure you are not holding them too long as you put them in the tray. Feed in small batches of fiber while you slowly turn the crank clockwise. Putting in a lot of fibers at once will jam the drums and the carder won't work properly. If that happens, you may have to turn the crank counterclockwise and remove the lump of fiber. Add fiber so that the big drum fills evenly, and don't let fluff fall over the sides and into the innards or chain.

When the teeth on the big drum are almost covered, it is time to take off the batt. Slide the **doffer** (a strong steel rod) into the seam on the big drum to lift up and separate the fibers. If you have a thick batt or longer fibers, you may have to work your way across the drum, lifting up sections at a time. Wool is amazingly strong!

Carefully peel the batt away from the drum and gently remove it from the carder; this first pass will not come off as cleanly as subsequent passes. Divide the batt into long strips and feed them into the carder again, spreading each section out to fit the drum. A batt that has been carded three times is usually well homogenized and free of clumps.

When the batt comes off the carder the final time, most spinners split it lengthwise and then pre-draft the strips into a light, lovely roving. Winding it into a neat bird's nest makes it ready to spin.

After you have finished using your carder, be sure to clean off both drums with a doffer brush. Use the doffer brush to gently lift off fibers from the drums, starting with the licker-in drum and then moving on to the big drum.

OTHER FIBER PREPARATIONS

There are a number of methods besides carding to prepare fibers for spinning; each is useful in its own way to produce a type of yarn. Here are a few simple, low-tech methods for preparing fiber that keep the lock structure intact.

Combing Fibers

Combed fibers have all the short fibers removed and the long fibers aligned to make smooth, strong yarn. Traditional wool combs are scary-looking things, with very long pointed teeth. You may want to learn to use those at some point, but basic combing can be done with a tool as simple as a dog comb.

1. Use a dog comb to comb out the end of the lock.

2. The combed lock is open and aligned.

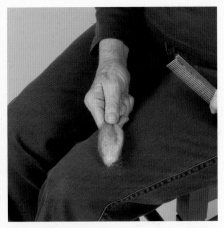

3. Flip the lock over and comb out the other end.

4. You could spin this lock as it is.

5. The short fibers and other undesirables stay on the comb.

Start with locks of wool at least 3 inches (7.5 cm) long. Hold one lock of wool firmly at one end and comb out the other end with a dog comb, keeping the wool in lock formation. Start combing at the tip of the fiber and work toward the center. When that end is combed out, flip the lock over and comb out the other end. The trick is to hold onto the lock firmly so you keep the fibers together. As you comb your fibers, be sure to place your locks so that they are all going in the same direction (all tip ends together).

Spin Combed Fibers

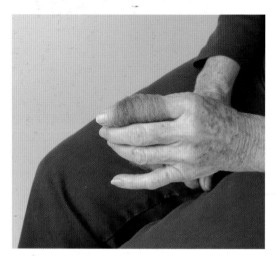

You could spin a lock over the fold.

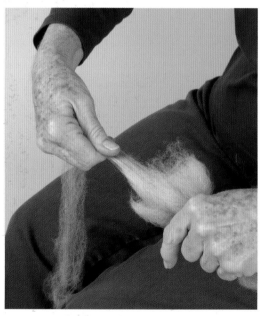

Holding several locks together, you could draft them into a tube of roving.

You can get the same effect using one handcard. Place a handcard in your lap. Hold a small lock of wool firmly at one end and draw the other end through the teeth of the card, pressing the fibers into the teeth with your other hand. Once one side is combed out, flip it over and comb out the other side.

You can spin this lock just as it is with a worsted draw (see page 81), spin it over the fold (see page 83), or add it to others and pull it into a roving if you want a worsted-style yarn. Of course, you can spin it any way you choose.

Flick Carding

A flick carder produces a preparation with properties somewhere between carded and combed. The fiber is still in lock formation, but some shorter fibers still remain. A yarn spun from flick-carded locks is smoother than a yarn spun from a rolag, but maintains some elasticity if spun woolen. Use this method with longer locks of wool (at least 4 inches [10 cm]) to open up the ends of the lock for easy spinning. Be sure to use a board or strong fabric to protect your leg from the flicker.

Hold a lock of wool by the cut end, resting the lock and your hand on your protected leg. Using a bouncing motion with the flicker, gently strike the tip end of the lock. Don't use the flicker as a comb; you are not trying to remove the shorter fibers, just open them up. As you tap the lock with the flicker, the fibers will pouf into an airy fan. After the tip end is fluffed, turn the lock around and open the cut end. You can spin these locks over the fold, straight out of your hand, or group several locks together and then pull a roving from them.

Flick Carding

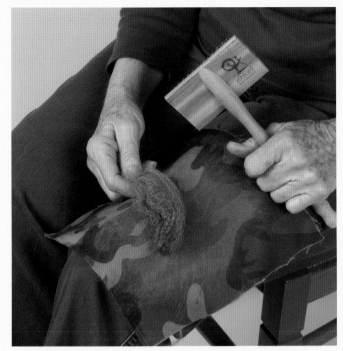

1. Hold the lock by the cut end against your protected leg.

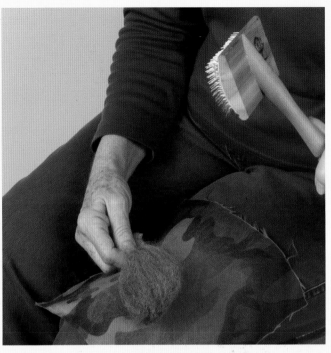

2. This lock is ready to be flick carded.

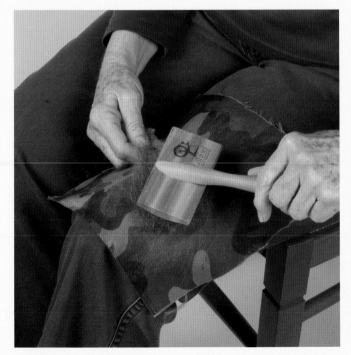

3. Tap the end of the lock with the flick carder—do not use it as a comb.

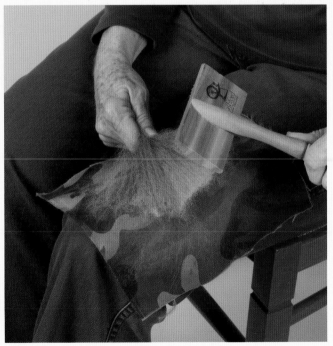

4. The flick-carded lock will open up into an airy fan.

Spinning Wheel Maintenance

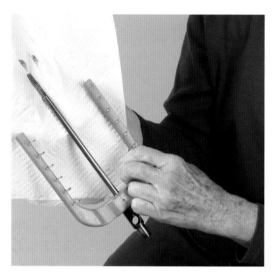

Wipe off the flyer with a paper towel.

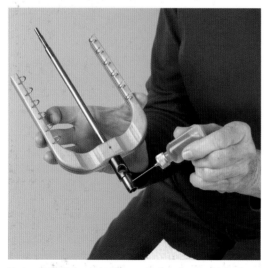

Put a little oil on the flyer shaft where the bobbin sits, at the orifice, and at the back maiden.

Remember my saying that choosing a spinning wheel is like choosing a car? Just like a car, your spinning wheel needs regular maintenance to keep it working properly. With proper care, your spinning wheel can last far longer than a car will, even if you use it every day and make miles of yarn.

Oil the Flyer

Like a car, the most frequent service your wheel needs is an oil change now and then to keep it running smoothly. It isn't hard—it just requires a paper towel and some oil, either 30-weight motor oil or sewing machine oil. Every time you change your bobbin, wipe off the flyer shaft and the orifice with a paper towel. Don't be surprised at the black gunk on the towel. Before you replace the bobbin, put a little oil on the flyer shaft where the bobbin sits, a drop where the orifice goes into the front maiden, and a drop at the back maiden. If part of the flyer is screwed on, don't oil the threaded area.

Oil and Clean the Wheel

Other parts of your wheel need care too, but not quite as often. The trick is to clean off the area and then add a little lubricant. Moving parts create an amazing amount of friction, so a little oil is a good thing. Unless your wheel has sealed bearings, put a drop of oil on each side of the drive-wheel hub and where the crank connects with the footman. Clean off the area where the treadle pivots occasionally and oil it, too. If you have leather parts, they also need lubrication, but not so much that they stretch out of shape. Try using a little furniture wax occasionally.

Dust and polish your wheel just as you would a fine piece of furniture. Don't polish the grooves where the drive band or brake band go; you want good contact between the wood and the drive band. Keep the wheel away from direct sunlight, heating vents, and fireplaces for long periods of time to prevent the wood from drying out and shrinking.

Now and then, clean out the core of your bobbins with a cotton swab and check that the bobbin ends are on tight. If the bobbin ends are loose, pull them off and reglue them with wood glue. Let them set for 24 hours before using them again. Check to see that the bobbins turn freely on the flyer shaft; if they don't, they may need to be reamed out or repaired. Check with the manufacturer for bobbin repair tips.

Drive and Brake Bands

Check your drive bands and brake bands for wear occasionally. If a cotton drive band gets worn or stretches out too much, replace it with a soft cotton package twine about the size of the manufacturer's band. (A thicker band may not fit the whorl groove.)

First adjust the flyer so you can tighten the drive band if it stretches. Use the mechanism that adjusts the flyer to move it is as close to the drive wheel as possible. Measure a new drive band by placing it around the drive wheel and flyer, leaving a little extra to tie the knot. You can splice the two ends of a drive band together by sewing them, or you can just tie a square knot. I'll admit I'm lazy and usually just tie a knot instead of sewing my drive bands. After tying the knot, test it for strength (did you really tie a square knot?). Now see how your wheel works. If the drive band is too tight, you may have to undo that square knot and make the band just the tiniest bit bigger. If the drive band is too loose, you can adjust your wheel to take up the slack. You should be able to treadle with ease. Once you have tested the band for strength and size, then you can clip off the loose ends of the knot. When you replace the band on a double-drive wheel, make sure the band only crosses itself only one time.

To replace adjustable drive bands, you will probably need to separate the footman from the drive wheel so you can switch bands. Check the manufacturer's instructions for specific details.

Brake bands may need repair too, when the string wears out or when the spring or the rubber band breaks. You can replace your brake band with a piece of linen or cotton yarn. If the spring on your brake band is stretched out of shape, get a new one from your supplier or use a rubber band as your tensioning device. The nice thing about using a rubber band is that it is easily available.

Your wheel should not have the wobbles. Vibration loosens everything over time, so tighten any loose screws or bolts.

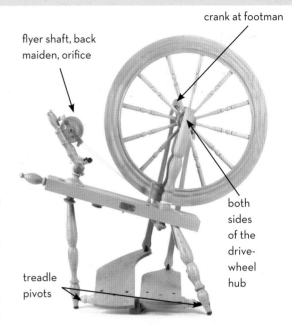

Where your wheel needs oil.

Oil both sides of the drive-wheel hub.

Clean and oil the treadle pivots.

Glossary

Batt—A rectangle of carded fibers made on a drumcarder.

Bradford Count—A system that describes the fineness of a fleece. The count refers to the number of 560-yard skeins that can be spun from one pound of wool top.

Brake band—A tensioning device on some wheels. With scotch tension the brake band is on the bobbin; with irish tension the brake is on the flyer.

Bobbin—The spool that fits on the flyer shaft of the spinning wheel and holds yarn.

Cotty wool—Wool that is matted and tangled while still on the fleece.

Crimp—The waves in a lock of wool. The size and shape of the crimp is determined by breed.

Doffer—A tool (strong steel rod) used to remove the batt from a drumcarder.

Double drive—A type of spinning wheel that uses one continuous drive band folded over on itself; one part of the band drives the flyer and the other drives the bobbin.

Drafting—The action of pulling and sliding fibers past one another just before the twist enters and turns the fibers into yarn.

Drafting triangle—The area where twist meets drafted fibers and yarn is formed.

Drive band—The band that transfers the power of the drive wheel to the spinning wheel flyer.

Drumcarder—A machine consisting of two or more drums that arranges fibers into a large rectangle **(batt)** of carded fibers.

Flick carder or flicker—A small paddle with short, fine wire teeth on one side used to open up locks of wool while keeping them in lock formation.

Flyer—The U-shaped part of a wheel including the metal shaft that holds the bobbin. The arms of the flyer have hooks or a thread guide to allow yarn to wind onto the bobbin evenly. The orifice is located at the front of the flyer.

Footman—The rod that connects the treadle to the drive wheel.

Handcards—Two paddles with short, fine wire teeth that are used to card fibers for making into rolags.

Indian or irish tension (bobbin lead)—A type of spinning wheel where the drive band turns the bobbin and a brake band sits the flyer.

Kemp—Coarse, short, and brittle fibers found in some fleeces.

Lazy kate—A tool used during plying that holds bobbins of yarn to be plied together on the wheel.

Leader—Yarn, usually plied wool, that is tied onto a spindle or bobbin and used to begin spinning.

Lock—A small bundle or clump of fibers within a fleece.

Maidens—The two uprights that hold the flyer and bobbin in place on a wheel.

Mother-of-all—The two maidens and base that support the flyer and bobbin on a wheel.

Niddy-noddy—A tool used to make a skein of yarn. It looks like a capital letter I with the top and bottom arms at right angles to one another.

Noil—Little bits of short tangled fibers that make lumps in yarn.

Orifice—The opening at the front of the flyer that guides the yarn onto the flyer arms.

Over the fold (or from the fold)—A technique for spinning combed fibers in which a lock or staple is folded over the index finger and yarn is spun from the fingertip.

Ply—To twist two or more spun yarns together. Plying is almost always done in the opposite direction from which the singles were spun. Also refers to the individual strands that make up a plied yarn.

Pre-drafting—A technique to make fibers easier to spin by gently pulling fibers out into a long continuous overlapping strand.

Rolags—A fiber preparation resembling a jelly roll that is made with handcards.

Roving—Fibers that have been carded and then drawn out into a long strand, sometimes with a slight amount of twist.

S-twist—Counterclockwise twist.

Scotch tension (flyer lead)—A type of spinning wheel where the drive band turns the flyer and a brake band sits on the bobbin.

Scouring—Washing fiber before spinning to remove dirt and grease.

Sett gauge—A tool marked off in inch increments to measure wraps per inch.

Singles—One strand of yarn, spun in one direction.

Skirt—The process of removing the really dirty matted areas from a fleece after shearing.

Sliver—Carded fiber that had been formed into a long strand.

Staple—A lock of wool.

Staple length—A term that refers to the length of a particular fiber. Cotton fibers are very short, silk fibers can be very long.

Tension knob—On a single-drive wheel, the knob that adjusts how quickly yarn is pulled onto the bobbin by changing the tension on the brake band.

Tippy wool—Wool with damaged or very fragile tips.

Top (combed top)—A long strand of equal-length fibers, with the shorter fibers removed and the remaining fibers parallel to one another.

Treadle—The foot pedal that moves the drive wheel on a spinning wheel.

Whorl—On a spindle, the part of the spindle that adds weight. Spindle whorls are usually a flat round piece, although some are round beads, squares, or other shapes. On a spinning wheel, the pulley on a flyer and or bobbin that holds the drive band.

Woolen—Yarn created from carded fibers and spun with twist between the hands.

Worsted—Yarn made from combed fibers and spun with no twist between the hands.

Z-twist—Clockwise twist.

Bibliography

BOOKS

Amos, Alden. *The Alden Amos Big Book of Handspinning*. Loveland, Colorado: Interweave Press, 2001.

Buchanan, Rita. *A Dyer's Garden*. Loveland, Colorado: Interweave Press, 1995.

———. *A Weaver's Garden*. Loveland, Colorado: Interweave Press, 1999.

Field, Anne. *The Ashford Book of Spinning*. Christchurch, New Zealand: Shoal Bay Press, 1992.

———. *Spinning Wool Beyond the Basics*. Christchurch, New Zealand: Shoal Bay Press, 1995.

Fournier, Nola, and Jane Fournier. *In Sheep's Clothing*. Loveland, Colorado: Interweave Press, 1996.

Gibson-Roberts, Priscilla. *Spinning in the Old Way*. Fort Collins, Colorado: Nomad Press, 2006. Previously published as *High Whorling*.

Hochberg, Bette. *Fibre Facts*. Santa Cruz, California: B. Hochberg, 1981.

———. *Handspindles*. Santa Cruz, California: B. Hochberg, 1977.

———. *Handspinner's Handbook*. Santa Cruz, California: B. Hochberg, 1978.

———. *Spin, Span, Spun*. Santa Cruz, California: B. Hochberg, 1979.

Ligon, Linda, ed. *Homespun, Handknit*. Loveland, Colorado: Interweave Press, 1988.

MacKenzie McCuin, Judith. *Teach Yourself Visually Handspinning*. Hoboken, New Jersey: Wiley Publishing, 2007.

Menz, Deb. *Color in Spinning*. Loveland, Colorado: Interweave Press, 2005.

Raven, Lee. *Hands On Spinning*. Loveland, Colorado: Interweave Press, 1987.

Ross, Mabel. *The Essentials of Handspinning*. Kinross, Scotland: Mabel Ross, 1987.

———. *The Essentials of Yarn Design for Handspinners*. Kinross, Scotland: Mabel Ross, 1983.

Varney, Diane. *Spinning Designer Yarns*. Loveland, Colorado: Interweave Press, 2003.

MAGAZINES
Handwoven
Interweave Crochet
Interweave Knits
Shuttle Spindle & Dyepot
Spin-Off
Wild Fibers

Acknowledgments

Thanks to the many people at Interweave who put this book together: Anne Merrow, editor and gentle shepherd of books; Ann Swanson for brilliant photography; and Carol Huebescher Rhoades for her keen eye and good suggestions. Special thanks to Laura Shaw Feit for her design of the book.

Thanks also to the other people who have made such a difference in my life and spinning: to Judy, business partner and best of friends, your encouragement has meant the world to me; to the wonderful Shuttles staff, thanks for all the support and laughter; to Gail, thanks for good advice and music, an unbeatable combination; to all the teachers I've taken classes from, thank you for sharing your knowledge and enthusiasm, especially Judith MacKenzie McCuin; to my students, thank you for letting me teach you—it has been a great pleasure and I have learned so much from you. Many thanks to the wonderful wool growers I have been privileged to know, especially Clyde and Sharon Vair, Rocky and Carolyn Payne, and Natali and Mardy Steinberg. Some of you are no longer with us and your presence is sorely missed. To all the spindle and wheel makers and fiber producers, thank you for providing us with incredible tools and the most amazing fibers to spin the yarn of our dreams; special thanks to Barry and Jane of Schacht Spindle Company; thanks to my muse, Roxana Bartlett, and to Sue Dowgiert, Ruth Hollowell, and Margaret Wahlin for showing that garments created with handspun are beauty unsurpassed; thanks to Debi Dodge and Connie Kephart for their lovely yarns.

Special thanks to my neighbor and great friend Rosalie for adopting us into the Majkowski clan. Thanks to my daughter, Marika, who knits me socks and samples and fills my life with joy. And last but certainly not least, thanks to Linda Ligon for creating Interweave Press; you have given us such a gift.

Index

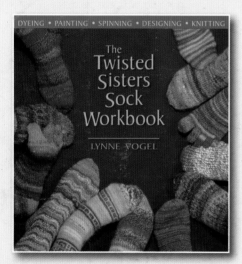

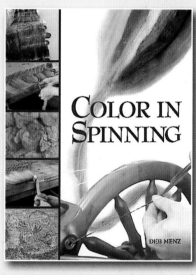